MW00878878

Praise for
Dear Alzheimer's: a caregiver's diary & poems

Poet Esther Altshul Helfgott chronicles her last seven years with her husband, pathologist Abe Schweid, in these devastating and redemptive diary entries and poems. Alzheimer's is an awful illness, but as Helfgott writes, "Poetry… is a way to understand the awfulness of life and to use that awfulness as a tool for growth and change." These intimate, powerful, brave poems are grounded in the searing fragmentary details of a caregiver's daily life. Our own participation in *Dear Alzheimer's*—in its mercy and its romance—is irresistible. Helfgott's gift is reminding us to live in spite of and because.

—Kathleen Flenniken
Washington State Poet Laureate 2012-2014
Author of *Famous* and *Plume*

If you know someone with Alzheimer's disease, you need this book, for it will shed much-needed insight into this devastating disease. If you don't, you'll still gain a deep appreciation for the power and tenacity of love and a visceral understanding of the need for compassion on this difficult path. *Dear Alzheimer's* is a unique and necessary addition to the growing shelf of literature about Alzheimer's disease.

—Holly J. Hughes
Editor, *Beyond Forgetting: Poetry and Prose about Alzheimer's Disease*

We must accept the truth that either our body or mind will outlive the other. Abe's wife Esther has captured the story of his ordinary body outliving his exemplary mind. The poems and journal descriptions of her husband's decline are as delicately made as one of Abe's slides, and as carefully examined. When we are advised that love is all there is, we should temper that comfort with the realization that someone has to die first. The cost for loving is suffering absence. Helfgott has exposed that painful reality with tenderness, honesty, and beauty.

—Richard Rapport, M.D.
Author of *Physician: The Life of Paul Beeson and Nerve Endings: The Discovery of the Synapse*

Esther's poems and diary entries immerse the reader into the complex, often heartbreaking world of the Alzheimer's caregiver. Her candor and willingness to share all aspects of the journey is inspiring. Like being in a good support group, readers will identify with Helfgott and gain perspective in their understanding of a spouse's life with Alzheimer's.

—Carin Mack, MSW
Geriatric Social Worker
Support Group Facilitator

From the opening sentence of Esther Helfgott's memoir, when her husband says, "I don't know where I am," the reader is pulled into this beautiful, raw, heart-wrenching account of their journey through Alzheimer's. This is a must read, not only for the millions of families affected by this horrific disease, but also for anyone dealing with the terminal illness of a loved one. Ms. Helfgott helps us learn that hardest lesson of all—how to let go and say goodbye.

—**Anne Serling**
    Author of *As I Knew Him: My Dad, Rod Serling*

Here in the only kind of language that will dare to enter imaginatively into its own, and our own disintegration—poetry—Esther teaches us what it means to have the courage to let go of what was, to let in what still is, and to let a new way of being us BE in the world. Entering into this dis-ease with Esther's imagination has awakened me to the inestimably precious gift that we give each other when we meet each other, in love, in the midst of life's unraveling.

—**Michael Verde**
    Founder and President of Memory Bridge: The Foundation for Alzheimer's and Cultural Memory

An honest and touching rendering of an intricate and personal time/space altering experience expressed beautifully in diary and poetry. This book offers great benefit to caregivers, friends and professionals whose lives have been touched by Alzheimer's disease.

—**Sandy Sabersky**
    Executive Director, ELDERWISE

This powerful and poignant memoir takes us through the labyrinth of loss and life that is Alzheimer's and in doing so it raises questions about the nature of 'self' and of relationship. The book is drenched in a beauty that comes out of prolonged but contained pain. It is a book to savor, one through which to meander with an open questioning mind, and a curiosity both about what it is like to be the carer of a loved one who struggles with a life changing event and what it is like to be the one who is changing.

—**Elisabeth Hanscombe**
  Unit for Studies in Biography and Autobiography,
  LaTrobe University, Melbourne, Australia

This book charts the inner life of caregiver as poet. Esther provides witness and a map into Abe's dementia. She says the diary has always been her friend. She offers us friendship and an open heart's knowledge. Their story guides us to understand what it means to love.

—**Gary Glazner**
  Founder, Alzheimer's Poetry Project

It takes a courageous person to write honestly and tenderly about the Alzheimer's journey. Esther's poetry does just that, taking us by the hand and leading us through the joys and sorrows of living life with a progressive, fatal disease.

—**Keri Pollock**
  Communications Director and Raconteur
  Alzheimer's Association Western and
  Central Washington State Chapter

洞月亮

CAVE MOON PRESS
YAKIMA 中 WASHINGTON

2013

Dear Alzheimer's

a caregiver's diary & poems

Dear Alzheimer's
a caregiver's diary & poems

For Lillian —
In peace & health
Love,
Esther

Esther Altshul Helfgott

洞月亮

CAVE MOON PRESS

YAKIMA 中 WASHINGTON

© Copyright 2013 Esther Altshul Helfgott
All rights reserved.
Photography by: Esther Altshul Helfgott
Book Design: Esther Altshul Helfgott and Doug Johnson

ISBN: 9781490572789

In Memory of Abe

Table of Contents

Dear Reader:

In August 2003, Abe and I were in the kitchen leaning over the counter reading the newspaper. All of a sudden, he stood up and looked out the window. He says:

I don't know where I am.

This has been coming "Where do you think you are?" I ask.

On Washington Avenue. I think I'll take the bus downtown.

Washington Avenue is in the Bronx. It's where Abe grew up.

I need to see some people, he says.

I don't tell Abe we're in Seattle, that he's lived here since the 1960s. In his mind he's in his childhood neighborhood; perhaps he's looking for his parents and their grocery store, the one his brother worked in and Abe always wanted to run away from. Maybe he's back there now. Helping his parents in a way he didn't then, when he went off to violin lessons or the Museum of Natural History and finally college and medical school, his brother and parents still working in the store.

I redirect him. We walk to the corner store to buy a *New York Times*. Now we're back in the kitchen in Ravenna where we've lived since 1987.

I've been putting off calling the doctor, but now I make an appointment.

Doctor says:
"We'll put him on Aricept
and you on *The 36 Hour Day: A Family Guide*
by Mace and Rabins.
See you in four months."

I might as well be holding a grizzly bear in my lap.

After the visit, we hold hands
I say: I'm confused a lot of the time.
What's the difference in our confusion?

When you're confused
you know you're confused, he says.
And that means you're not confused.

When I'm confused
I don't know
I'm confused
and that means
I am
confused.

. . . and squeezes my hand.

From an early age, my diary was my best friend. As an adult, poetry became my friend, as well. Both writing forms were especially useful to me as I sought to understand the progression of my husband's Alzheimer's disease. Writing offered me an outlet for the self-absorption I needed to prepare, on a daily basis, even on a minute-to-minute basis for the around-the-clock job of caregiving. If I had not allowed myself time to relax into a space that accelerated awareness of my interior life, I would not have been in shape to cope with the struggles Abe and I faced as we dealt with this ravaging disease.

The diary is an especially helpful writing tool because it is geared most naturally to the fragmented life, and I, who have experienced the fragmentary life of motherhood coupled with illness and divorce, still cannot imagine a life more intellectually fragmented than one affected by the throes and challenges of Alzheimer's. Here, in this diary, which has always been my document of life as battlefield, I not only work through conflicts concerning caregiving and self, but I also record my husband's memories. He and I had, in a sense, at that nadir in his life, become each other's writing partners. I became his memory and amanuensis and he the one who determined exactly what it was I would write at a given time.

How could I not grab a pen, for instance, and record his thoughts, when he awakened from a nightmare, his brother chasing him in a dream. He is ten years old and in the Bronx. He is not a retired Seattle pathologist looking through a microscope to see if a patient's cells are cancerous and I am not an independent poet and writer. My story is his, as well as mine, and my diary holds us both. It is filled with representations of our daily life, representations that may help others understand their own sorrows that are connected to this disease. But mostly, my diary helped me record and remember my husband and me in that scary and very crazy-making time.

I hope that while learning something about one couple's experience with Alzheimer's, these entries will help you understand the disease better. I also hope you won't have to come closer to it than these pages, and I thank you for following along with me.

2004

October 8, 2004

Reading Noah

I wakened this morning knowing that I had to tease out that which brought me to the story Abe and I have made together. And I remembered the first time I saw him in *shul* (synagogue)—not in Rabbi Ira Stone's class on Conservative Judaism where we met—but in the sanctuary.

And I saw him across the aisle from me, a man with a high forehead that looked as if it were bursting with knowledge that I didn't have and needed, a man in a loose cardigan sweater with a whale pin on the collar, a small man whose shoulders seemed to carry the world. So I got him out of bed before 11 a.m. and I cried with him to let me hear his voice again, the one he used to use reading Torah and *davening* (praying), rocking back and forth on the *bima* (dais), to tunes I didn't know my body always knew.

And he got up out of bed and I didn't nudge him to get dressed and he had a good breakfast which I put in front of him and I found him the old Book he used to read in *shul* and he sat down and studied *parsha* Noah, (the part of Genesis that holds Noah) because this was the time of year to read and study Noah. And he read to me, first in Hebrew, then he translated, and this is (some of) what we learned:

You may speak the whole of a person's praise in his or her absence but not in his or her presence and you do not utter a person's blame in his or her presence. Which must mean: one can speak praise of a person in his or her absence but not blame, and since one can't blame in the person's presence or absence, we are instructed in *parsha* Noah not to blame at all. (Based on an interpretation of the Yiddish Women's Bible, the *tz'enah ur'enah*.)

-1-

December 13, 2004

I imagine

he sees his father's grocery store in the Bronx and the apartment behind where he slept in the hall with his brother, Sam, their rooms having been let to boarders.

I imagine Abe and Sam hiding under their bed, while police collect Protection Money so their father, Henry, can keep his store open on Sundays.

And I imagine Abe searches for Regina, his mother, when she left him on a chair in Alexander's

department store—149th and 3rd Ave—while she sold bundles of clothes door to door. And now, going home, Abe eyes the ground as Regina pushes him under the subway turnstile.

I imagine Abe looking back at neighborhood ruffians who beat him up for being a Jew-boy.

And I see him watching his parents read letters from Europe, 1937. And as I see him wincing

in his chair, trying to reposition himself. I wonder if he was ever at home here.

October 9, 2004

Are you healthy

is what they ask me
when they see my hair
cut short
as if it had fallen out
from radiation treatments
and now grown back
in a stubble
spiked with pomade.

Always in surprise

I say, "Yes, I'm healthy,"
and they nod in their thinking
I'm a lie.

2005

April, 2005

Serendipity at a Poetry Therapy Workshop, St. Louis, MO: We're Instructed to Interview the Person Sitting Next to Us

—for Norma Leedy and in memory of Jack Leedy, founder of the National Association for Poetry Therapy

There must have been
an angel
sitting here
between us
waiting for our pens
to meet
over husbands'
slipping minds.

Jack's forty-five years
of patients
and poetry.

Abe's forty-five years
of oncology and
microscopes—
cell after cell
of stun-
ning
destruction

Two doctors' wives
reeling.

Dear Alzheimer's:

   Why
did you pick our
sheltered
lives
to
visit?

April 30, 2005

He Says

I'm so weary, so overwhelmed
by the weariness.
I rub his toes, his feet.
Ahhh, that feels good, he says
but then I begin deep muscle massage
and *no no, too much pressure,*
he says. I go gentle again,
and he relaxes back into himself
Do you want to come down for breakfast?
Oh, no, that's the last thing I want.
My hips, my legs. My thighs.
I can't get up today. I don't know why
I'm so weary. Are you hungry?
No, no. I'm weary,
so weary. . .

May 15, 2005

Shopping with Alzheimer's

I didn't know where you were
he hid his face
I was waiting for you
all through the vegetables
It's confusing here
and even the fruit

June 9, 2005

Mercy

This morning I wanted to set up the Orion Telescope CD for Abe, the one that came with the telescope I gave him for his 76th birthday last year, but every time I try to get him to use the computer, even if it doesn't concern email or the internet, he turns his nose up, as if it comes from a different world, and indeed, it does. I've thought I could tempt him with science since he's a retired pathologist and ever since he was a kid, went to the Bronx High School of Science, won the Westinghouse Science Talent Search Award and I don't know how many others, he has been hypnotized by all things science. But now his eyes go elsewhere, and I give up the notion of learning more about planetary systems with him, at least for today. I start to get up to do the dishes, but his words stop me:

This room has so much mercy in it

I sit back down. What do you mean?

The goodness of it . . .

Hmmm?

the books, the words
that fall from the shelves

The quiet. . . the softness. . . and poetry
The whole aura of this place

With Bach playing in the background?

Yes and the bananas. . .
There's a certain tenderness in bananas

In the oatmeal
with the milk poured over it?

Yes, and the picture in front of the Freud books
it has a certain peacefulness to it

The one of you and Butchie?

Yes, on the porch,
in the sun.
We're almost praying

Praying?

Yes, praying. . .
for things future. . . for things past. . .

I've always thought of the kitchen table in our library/family/every-
thing-in-it room as a crowded mess. Not until now and this conversa-
tion with Abe, tired and infirm, have I considered that there could be
anything as grand or as simple as mercy here in our scrambled lives.

August 12, 2005

I can't finish my ideas.
My words are upside down.
When I begin an idea,
it's not there when I go back to it
            —Abraham I. Schweid, M.D.

4:00 p.m.

And after Adult Day Care, he says:

It was the most dramatic
of days,
with nice people
trying
to get to know
each other
sit situation
    but

August 23, 2005

Suzzallo, a place of worship

the library is the soul of the university
—Henry Suzzallo (1875-1933)

I can't
remember
when it was
the last time
I walked
these stacks.
The smell
of nineteenth-
century
tomes:
the sound
of dark-
ness. The touch
of cracked
leath-
er. The taste.
Up
and down
the aisles
of centuries.
The feel
of dead
people
seeing
me.

September 7, 2005

Alzheimer's is

                getting lost
in your neighborhood.
It's sitting at the bus stop
quarter-to-one in the morning,
your wife running
up
and down
the alley
screaming a name
you don't know is yours.
Alzheimer's is
getting lost
between the floors
of your own home,
the one your salary
paid for. It's
forgetting
the names of the bones in the body
never mind you were
a pathologist
and spent a lifetime
examining them.
Alzheimer's is
un-
learning
what you always knew.
It's losing yourself.
It's asking your wife:

What
business
was
I
in?

Ha Tikvah (the Hope)
—for Billy and Sharon

Abe cries when he sees a picture of our cousin Billy on his way to making *Aliyah*. He wants to go too, not just because his father is buried in the military cemetery—in Nahariya—next to his cousin who died in the '48 war, but because Israel is the (mythical) homeland he grew up with *schlepping* books and blue and white tin cans from one bus stop in the Bronx to another, boarding New York trolleys with *pushkas* the UJA (United Jewish Appeal) distributed in his Tremont Avenue Hebrew school. As he thinks of Billy leaving, Abe listens to the sound of coins dropping like small metal matzo balls in the pot on his mother's old stove. In his ears, a melody of hope, *Ha Tikvah*, and of Israel where his parents didn't settle where his aunt and uncle, pioneer *kibbutzniks,* did settle and where his grandparents would have settled if not for—

October 2, 2005

Mary Oliver's Bone

Today, I read him Mary Oliver's *Bone*.
He loves it so, he cries
until tears

fall

in his mouth
and flood the soul she

searches for   in the ear bone
of the pilot whale
she finds
in Provincetown.

In Seattle,
her book re-

turned
to our shelf
I fold
us into

each other's

bodies
as we sleep
in the
long
wet
night.   -18-

October 10, 2005

Movies I've Watched This Week

The Sea of Grass (1947)
drama/western
Hepburn and Tracy

The Locket (1946)
film-noir
Laraine Day, Robert Mitchum, Brian Aherne

To Have and Have Not (1944)
thriller
Bogart and Bacall, Walter Brennan

Dangerous (1935)
drama
Bette Davis, Franchot Tone

October 11, 2005

Nobody knows what to do
including/especially the doctors
who want me to bring him for an appoint-
ment. They have no idea
what it means
to get him dressed
and into a car
to take him
to an
appointment.
He needs a hospital bed
not an appointment.

October 12, 2005

This morning, his language

skills are good
and he uses them
to the utmost.

In the shower,
he yells:
Let me out of here!

Dressing him,
he pouts:
I can't wear that.

Fixing his hair,
he says:
You're

tearing
holes in my scalp.
Every time
you brush
my
head hurts.

I suppose,
I need
to find a gentler
faucet,
and a softer
brushing hand,
one with the child
still in it.

October 29, 2005

More

All the while
he loses language
he develops
the ability
to find
and use words
that duplicate his
emotions.

In this awful season of rain,
he's found a new way
of learning,
of teaching himself
more about himself
and his seventy-seven years
of living.

In so doing, this moment
in our lives together

gifts me
gifts him
gifts us

with unraveling questions
and apostrophes
between us.

This new use of language

         the mumblings   and ramblings

(that others think are meaningless un-
                hooked together sentences of
drivel)

contains answers I have looked for

throughout our twenty-

five year-old
marriage bed.

Now, indecipherable speech

breathes more

ness
into our un-

used-up lives.

November 3, 2005

Alzheimer Couple

They have grown
into each other
like two plants
in a small pot.
Arms and legs
encircling
the same
trunk
they wait
for anyone
to come
and water
them.

November 4, 2005

Tonight

I admit he can no longer read
all the while he sits at the table
bent over his paper
poised to read.

I ask him:
What's happening?

The
words
won't to my cortex,
he says.

Stick? I ask.

Yes,
stick.

The
words
won't
to
my
cortex

Swee
har
t

November 4, 2005

As I Sit In Class

I think of him wanting to come home, how I pinned my business card to his undershirt. On the back I wrote: "You're in Adult Day Care. I'm going to class. I'll pick you up at 1:30 p.m."

He reads the words with me—aloud. I kiss him goodbye, give the nurse a plastic baggie filled with Tylenol and a just-in-cast Ativan.

In class, the students and I write and talk about writing. We read Bill Stafford's *What's In My Journal* as my cellphone sits unringing by the door.

November 8, 2005

Ativan, a Blessing?

After two weeks
of sleep
deprivation
for both of us
I give him the Ativan
and get a whole night's sleep.
(Well, almost).
And so does he.
(Well, almost),
but he wobbles in the morning.
(At least).
And getting up from a chair
is har
der.
And in adult care
he sleeps,
so they'll
keep him there.
Until
I pick him up
and night
begins
again, as day
doesn't.

November 10, 2005

Mistakes

I worry about turning right when I might have turned left, letting him
sleep instead of getting him up for breakfast, following his lead when
I might have stood firm in my instructions to shower, dress, eat, go
for a walk with Hassan, the Kenyan caregiver who watches over him
and the house when I'm gone.

He is somewhat better today as he used to be all the while needy for
old times: he cries for mother, father gone fifty years brother-issues
unresolved. There is no peace in this man, not this morning
not today. Really, Esther, your mistakes don't matter.

November 16, 2005

Laboratory Visit

The first time I see him hold a colon, blood dripping through fingers of his latex gloves, I want to run away from the laboratory and the team of hovering technicians, this one handing him a scalpel that one, the scissors he took from home. But instead of running as I want to, and I really, really want to, I slump outside the door as he cuts. The procedure ends and we return to his office with the sign "Dr. Schweid" on the door. I watch him change from his white lab coat to a tweed sports jacket in time for our lunch and the veggie sandwich I can't touch.

November 17, 2005

The Old Pathologist

I hold him
in my arms
as if he were
the remnants
of the baby au-
topsy he did
that day
in 1990
when I lost
those forty pages
of my writing
to the broken hard drive.
And looked, as he said,
as stricken
as the infant's mother
when the doctor said:
Your child is dead.

Now his head in my lap,
I stroke his brow and kiss his lips
while tears fill our
mouths
as we gasp for sounds of one more
tomorrow
and give us back our yesterdays.

November 26, 2005

No Ativan This Night, He's Home With Me

He did not need an Ativan last night.
He did not need restraint,
even redirection.
He was with me
here at home
sleeping comfortably
in his own bed.

Bessie Burton's Alzheimer's
unit is supposed to be one of the best
in the city. I beg your pardon.
I doubt if there is a best
in any city when speaking
of Alzheimer's.
There is no differentiation
between high functioning, as Abe is,
and low functioning
where people take their clothes
off in the halls, need constant redirection
and restraint.

Is it not the psychotropic drugs
that psychiatrists and drug companies
push down our throats—all our
throats—
to keep us *out of danger*
as they say,

that make Alzheimer's patients
that way in the first place,
instead of calming them down,
as they're supposed to do.

I could not leave him in that place of horror
where people are doped
up and warehoused
without concern
for individuality.

He didn't need Ativan last night
and I doubt if he needed it in the hospital.
What he needs, of course:
lips on the forehead
a back massage
and the strength that I give him.
As I gave to my children
(even as a single parent)
and to my mother (or tried to).
And I can give it to him,
even more than I did them.
Because I am, believe it or not—
it is true—wiser
for the age
I have been given,
so far.

May age be for a blessing
instead of a curse.
Amen.

November 29, 2005

Reading with Alzheimer's

Sprawled out
in the recliner
wearing
a tie-dyed shirt
the kids
gave him,
a Middle Eastern
yarmulke
on his head,
he holds
a book of stories
in his hands,
turns
the pages
as he always did:
carefully,
respectfully,
leaning, learning
words the brain loses
before he under-
stands.

December 14, 2005

Death, the Unholy

Long before he should have, he eluded decisions about his death. He'd say: *I'll never die.* This from a man who did autopsies nearly every day.

He didn't want to tend a mirage of promised and unimagined pleasure where he knew there was none, only unwritten codes and directions to a nonexistent thoroughfare.

Now, he looks back on unfilled spaces, especially those that held the word Yes, and in no uncertain terms, he says: *Death is unholy. Unholy. Profane. In its lack.*

2006

January 4, 2006

Abe was delighted to hear that Dov called, really perked up. He said come any time. I told Dov I start back teaching at Cancer Lifeline Monday so he'll be at Elder Health from 10- 3 Mondays, Wednesdays, Fridays. He's usually most alert during those hours but he's fine tonight. Just depends on. . .who knows. . .the brain makes up its own mind.

April 10, 2006

Early Morning Fragment

I awaken this morning feeling fat and lax.
I don't know how long we can go on this way,
how long I can. Holding on is the ripple,
the small sound, the slip of a turn or move-
ment, the hope in the night.
But ripples dissipate. They fade.
And what remains is chore,
the same as yesterday:
getting him up
for breakfast news-
paper, forget the change of clothes
the shower, just get him fed. . .

This is an early morning fragment.
I'll finish later when a ripple
returns.

April 13, 2006

Alzheimer's or not, it's Pesach

I am from a place of long ago
where women held timbrels
and danced by the sea.
My name is not Miriam
and Moses was not my brother
but I carry their rhythm
within me
and we hold hands
as I sing.

April 25, 2006

Evening walk

I went for a walk in the neighborhood last night and paid witness to the tulips and periwinkles. He was sitting in his chair watching television when I left. Our new live-in helper was with him. They had just turned on 60 Minutes when I walked out the door. This was the first time in I-don't-know-how-long I was able to go for a walk by myself after dinner, and at first I thought the world had changed. But when I came home an hour later and saw him sitting in that same spot, with the same affect, I felt the old familiar sadness return, the same sadness I felt a few hours earlier when I was taking his blood pressure and realized that he no longer understood the meaning of the numbers I was reading. When I got him to bed I thought I would work at my writing but my mind will not go there. It's in bed with him/wondering/what language Alzheimer's dreams in.

June 13, 2006

Note to self

9:00 a.m.

Saw three facilities yesterday and will contact more today.
As I study institutions, I can't imagine placing him.
Yet, when we got into bed last night,
he didn't even know he was home.

This can't be home, he said.

"Where are you?" I asked.

In the hospital, he said.

He knows more about what's happening than I do.

10:00 p.m. same day

I've been in huge denial.
Tomorrow is his birthday.
I ask him what he wants.
He says *peace.*

June 15, 2006

M. asks me what nursing facilities I visited this week. She lives in West Seattle.

I tell her I haven't visited in West Seattle but a friend's mother-in-law's in a facility there and she likes it. I'll ask her.

I visited St. Anne's in North Seattle, which seemed good, 47 beds and clean atmosphere. I was not in the patient area so didn't see staff-patient interaction and didn't ask about ratios. They don't have a locked facility.

Then I went to Aegis, where they only check on the patients every two hours. There's an elevator which patients go on themselves. I didn't like that.

Then to Evergreen, an adult family home where about eight patients were sitting on couches, mouths open, sleeping or staring at a turned-off television. I was out of there in a hurry. No male beds anyway.

I don't want him in a locked facility, but in the past he's wandered. He doesn't now but an admissions person at another facility, Foss, told me that when my husband gets away from me he will be upset and will want to leave where he is. Probably true, so at this point I'm thinking to hire more people at home until he no longer knows me. Lousy break for people who paid so much dues, huh? For anyone. I'm sick of K's Pollyanna attitude where everything's good if you make it so.

Summer 2006

The Almost Widow

I have read in a number of places that a woman married to a man with Alzheimer's is living a widow's life. In the two-and-a-half years since my husband's diagnosis, I have not felt a sense of widowhood, but last night at a social function I did feel I am living the life of an almost widow. Here at the table were a handful of couples, each, while engaged with everyone in the group as I was, were also happily engaged with each other.

I went to the function myself because I knew it would be too stressful and too late at night for Abe. We have in-home care now so I pushed myself to go. I had a wonderful time, actually, meeting new people and visiting with long-time associates, but I missed my husband and felt myself bringing up his name in conversation a little too often. It worked out fine, but now that I am able to get out of the house and explore myself in new territories, I need to figure out how I am going to handle myself as an almost widow.

It is not that I haven't been independent during our twenty-five years of marriage, traveling, working, socializing and maintaining my own friendship networks, but now the rules are different. Whereas pre-diagnosis, and even earlier (since he probably had the disease long before I or the doctors knew) I left the house independently with the knowledge that he knew what to do with his own time.

Now, in Stage 5 Alzheimer's, my husband's initiative is gone, as is his possibility for arranging or participating in a social life, or simply scheduling a few hours of errands. I arrange his day and another caregiver is with him when I am not. I help him with personal care, meals and all activities. His freedom is pretty much gone. Often, I feel that mine is too. Still, we manage, with pleasant moments weaving in and out of those that exhaust us both.

Mourning the Relationship

By the time I realized I had settled into the role of spousal caregiver, my role had changed to include the experience of mourning the relationship that, for better or worse, had been. Getting out as an almost widow, whether to a poetry reading, a concert or an art exhibit, was not going to be as easy as buying a ticket or calling some friends. I was taking the Alzheimer relationship with me, leaving at least three quarters of myself at home with my husband's silent gaze.

I have been attending support groups for Alzheimer's caregivers for a while and have been participating in the online Alzheimer's community. Both are helpful, but in each a component has been missing for me: discussions of grief and a focus on mourning before an actual death. And with Alzheimer's death is a daily occurrence.

When my mother was dying from heart disease, I attended a grief group at Northwest hospital. It provided a helpful outlet for expressing the feelings that come with knowing your loved one (LO) is in the process of dying, unlike the Alzheimer groups I have attended where the focus is often on the LO's behaviors.

Not everyone needs support groups, but, for me, they work toward helping me analyze and understand the grief process. When I leave my home, grief is my escort. Music, writing, and art may soothe, but none of those media help me shake off the feelings of mourning and grief. I know this about myself. So I google grief groups, Seattle hospitals, churches and synagogues and find the numbers I am looking for.

An almost widow is not a widow. The relationship that used to be has taken a different form, but wherever I go, Abe and his illness are with me.

August 2006

Part 2

Assisted Living Facility

August 16, 2006

The next twenty-four hours are not mine.
They belong to a place I've never been,
one with filling out admittance forms
and packing up his things,
a pair of pants here, a memory there.
Then the shirts and socks.
Shoes, toothbrush, underwear. I can't forget
his handkerchiefs, hand soap or comb.
I don't know what to put them in:
an overnight bag or suitcase. . .
And, then, the photos: him and me,
the children, for the wall.

August 17, 2006

Today Abe moved to an assisted living facility.

August 22, 2006

He'd always been reading, and still is, but yesterday, when I asked him if he wanted a newspaper he said, *No! What do I need it for. All that crap in there.* And on the day we were driving to the Assisted Living Facility for the first time, when I said, "Oh, I forgot to bring some books," he said: *Good, I don't need the pressure.*

The floor-to-ceiling books in the house must have filled him with anxiety, a look back to a life that he could no longer grasp. This hadn't occurred to me.

August 24, 2006

A Magazine Article Asks:
What's the best thing to happen to you this week?

- Seeing Abe enjoy activities and people at the Assisted Living Facility
- Watching him smile at other residents as they walk by
- Listening to him say hello to the man across the way
- Watching him shake someone's hand
- Seeing him with a group of staff and residents at a nurse's baby shower
- Hearing him say he's having a good time

August 30, 2006

Before he went to assisted living, sometimes at night when he was most confused, he would walk around the house looking for Esther. *Where's Esther?* he'd ask. "I'm here," I'd say. He'd smile and say, *I'm so glad.*

September 4, 2006

Alzheimer's As Prayer

Who would have thought
that Alzheimer's
would knit
the warmest and best parts
of our struggle together
into a blanket
and like a prayer
hold it over us
until
morning
came?

January 2007 – June 10, 2010

Part 3

Nursing Home

2007

January 14, 2007

Letter to Alzheimer's Association Online Community, Caregiver Forum

It's been months since I've stopped here. Abe's been in assisted living since August 17th and I am just now learning to accept our new living arrangements. It's strange being in the house without him and I've been going through a stage of "shall I sell the house or not sell." I'm over that and plan to stay put, at least for now.

Abe has adjusted beautifully. His doctor skills kicked in almost immediately and whether or not he remembers his doctoring days he's using what he knew to look out for people in his new community. He welcomes newcomers and does his best to show them the ropes.

He's become peaceful, content at times. I leave him with a sense of pride in his well-being and feel blessed that he's been able to gather himself up into a new or revised self with grace. I try to be as well-balanced as he has become, but frankly adjusting hasn't been easy for me.

Now, however, in the start of this new year, I am turning a corner and coming out of myself, having friends over, going out a little and getting back to my writing and teaching. So I'm here to send greetings and to say hello again.

It's good to see your names on the screen and read about your lives. I hope to catch up with what's been going on with you and wish you all a Happy New Year.

February 19, 2007

Primo Levi

I'm still reading Primo Levi. This time *The Drowned and the Saved*. I realize that comparing illness to a concentration experience is invalid, perhaps even unjust, but Concentration Camp literature is helping me conceptualize Alzheimer's more than anything I've read on Alzheimer's. For instance, "...our ability to decide had been amputated. Therefore we are not responsible and cannot be punished." (p. 29)

I think of how often Alzheimer patients are punished for "bad behavior," *e.g. I don't want to take a shower. Leave me alone,* and given drugs to modify that behavior so personnel can get their work done. On the one hand, understandable; on the other, a ratio of one care worker to fifteen patients is untenable.

One day Abe raised his cane at a resident who was bothering him and right away the head nurse wanted to put him on drugs. "Except for Abe, they're almost all on Depakote," another nurse said. I spoke to the doctor and a resident's daughter and that's not at all true. Meanwhile, the cane raising hasn't happened again and he didn't have to go on drugs. Plus, that person has let him alone.

March 30, 2007

I want to bring him home today, just for a visit

I called the facility and let the caregiver know that I would be there early and could they have him ready to go out. It was 9:00 a.m.; he hadn't wanted breakfast and was still in bed. I spoke to him on the phone, and he got right up. When I arrived he was sitting on our loveseat smiling. I said, "Come on, it's a beautiful day. Let's go for a ride." He was delighted.

We drove the scenic back roads so he could see the cherry blossoms, and on the way we stopped to pick up bagels and cream cheese sandwiches for lunch. He went into the deli with me, sat while I waited in line and enjoyed the comings and goings of the customers. When we pulled up to the house, he recognized it, I think, unbuckled his seatbelt and came inside with me. I took him up the elevator which he found comfortable but did not recognize. (Maybe he was in a fog even then, four years ago, when we were having it built). And we sat down at the table to eat our sandwiches.

Afterwards he sat in his recliner. I flipped on the switch to the gas fireplace and he watched the flames. I put on Mozart, curled up on the couch, and watched him watch the flames. I felt as if a world I used to know had returned to our living room and all of a sudden, after all these seven long months, the house—with him in it—made sense again.

Finally the bathroom called and afterwards we went outside for a walk, about half a block, and he was tired. And I was tired watching him be tired and I took him home, collected our things, watched him not say goodbye to the dog and got us in the car. When we arrived back at the facility, he smiled at the people who greeted him. He wanted to sit down. I watched him sit down. Sat next to him for a while, then kissed him goodbye and went home.

April 6, 2007

Can we meet for dinner, he asks when I call at 4:50, right before his supper hour. It doesn't matter that I was there yesterday and we loved as we could love.

I know I shouldn't ask him, "Do you remember I was there yesterday?" but I forget and ask him anyway and thus I speak more of me than of him.

My words roll right by us as he asks again, *Can we meet for dinner?*

I am shamed back into his reality and say to him, "Tomorrow, tomorrow for lunch, we'll meet tomorrow for lunch." He is more than satisfied, says, *That will be just fine. What time should we get together?* as if he's asking for a date. I say, I'll pick you up at noon and he says, *I'll try to make it.* Is he playing hard to get? Is he? How can the heart not break?

There are those who say: "You're not getting anything back. You need to move on and find a new life for yourself." And I wonder why they think I don't get anything back when learning Alzheimer Speak is as good as going for another Ph.D. Or looking in the mirror. To find myself inside the other.

April 9, 2007

I miss me,
   he said.

I miss you too

April 20, 2007

I'm afraid I'll die before he does. Who will take care of him? Should I really fly off to NY?

April 24, 2007

I'm on a plane to NY.

June 12, 2007

My article was published in The *Seattle Post-Intelligencer* today. I hope I'm not betraying him. It was on the editorial page. Maybe he would be proud. I was a Guest Columnist. Here it is:

You can improve quality of life for Alzheimer's patients.

You don't get anything back, a friend said after I came home from a visit with my husband. Maybe you shouldn't see him so much, another said. It's true that my husband's illness is not pleasant and my reaction after seeing him is not always upbeat, but so what.

I didn't jump for joy years ago when my youngest son had to be hospitalized multiple times for asthma. No one told me then that my child didn't give me anything back or that I shouldn't go to see him. On the contrary. Had I not been able to care for my asthmatic child, criticism certainly would have followed, from others as well as myself. Human beings give something back regardless of the physical or mental condition they are in. They teach us, if we let them, greater understanding of the human condition. And they teach us about ourselves.

My husband, Abe, has been living in an assisted living facility since August. He was diagnosed with Alzheimer's disease a few years before. After caring for him in our home for four years, first by myself and then with a host of caregivers, including one live-in, the disease overwhelmed us both. Last summer after I kept getting sick, I moved him to a memory care center that is architecturally structured so he can wander but not get lost.

Abe has adjusted well to the move. Most of his needs are met, he's safe and he is part of a community that accepts him for who he is now. But some who come to visit do not see Abe. They see a disease. They are disappointed when he does not engage in everyday conversation. They would like to take him to lunch or dinner. Otherwise, what is there to do with him, one asks, just sit there? I would suggest, yes, sit and engage in a new kind of listening. Abe has aphasia, a characteristic of Alzheimer's. He can't access language the way he used to and can't be expected to have an ordinary conversation. But plenty of neurons are still working, and the mind, which is a subjective manifestation of the brain, makes good use of them.

Take a walk around the facility or join an activity the staff provides. Interact with the other residents. If a woman approaches you and says she's waiting for a bus and asks where it is, tell her you don't know, or it's Sunday so it won't be coming today. Go with wherever the person is at the moment. You aren't lying. You're respecting that resident's here and now. Be in the moment with Alzheimer's sufferers. That's where they are. Don't pressure them with questions or for facts they can no longer remember. Have patience.

Stan Zeitz has. He and Abe study Hebrew together. When I thank him for continuing to visit, Stan says, "I get as much back from Abe as he gets from me. He may not say a word, but the minute I make a mistake in the Hebrew, he is on the spot correcting me. He still has an amazing facility for prayer and Hebrew text." Just as he has for reading poetry and listening to me read to him.

Your visit will not cure any one of the five million Americans living with Alzheimer's—but it will increase the quality of an Alzheimer sufferer's life for a little while longer. To my way of thinking, that's getting something back.

June 24, 2007

He still seems to know when I talk to him about him and me, not so much the things we did together, but the camaraderie. It's still there. We can still curl up together.

August 14, 2007

Second Guest Editorial, The Seattle P.I.

Caregiver's 'village' not big enough

When I read about the mother/daughter murder-suicide at Evergreen-Washelli Cemetery on July 24, my back went up. As far as I knew, those women were strangers to me, but their ages—the daughter 60 and the mother 92—made me wonder if this was not a caregiver situation gone wrong—and lots of caregiving situations go wrong.

How can they not when care generally falls on the emotional and physical shoulders of one person, usually a spouse or a daughter, but on sons as well. Whoever the caregiver, whatever the gender, caregivers suffer alongside their loved ones.

According to the Alzheimer's Association, "One in eight Alzheimer caregivers becomes ill or injured as a direct result of caregiving, and one in three uses medication for caregiving-related problems."

Before my husband, who has Alzheimer's, was moved into a facility, I was a caregiver who fell into both of those categories. I am still one of those statistics and want to emphasize that caregiving does not stop once the patient leaves home. New problems arise that fall on the backs of primary caregivers.

I did not know the circumstances surrounding the tragedy of the two women, beyond what was reported. They were found shot in the head. The mother was dead and the daughter was hospitalized at Harborview Medical Center in critical condition. She died five days later. A gun had been found in her lap and police presumed that the daughter shot the mother and turned the gun on herself. The mother's death was ruled a homicide.

I was fast to speculate: Did the mother want to die? Was the killing assisted suicide? Was the daughter a primary caregiver? She had picked up her mother from a Lynnwood assisted living center. Those facilities are usually private pay. Had the family's money run out? Why did the daughter have a gun? What were the dynamics of the mother-daughter relationship?

The next day when I was getting ready to visit my husband, I received a call from the director of the memory care facility where he lives. She wanted to let me know, presumably before I heard it anywhere else, that the woman killed in the car at Washelli lived in the same cottage as my husband.

Certainly, I knew who she was. We had exchanged smiles at least twice a week. She always had rouge on. I never met the daughter. We visited at different times. She came around the supper hour and I in the early afternoon. I do not know why she killed her mother and then herself, but she was, indeed, a caregiver.

Like homelessness, illness in old age is a societal problem. Heaping the burden of care onto one person or even individual families is not realistic for many reasons. Sometimes, for instance, family members are not equipped psychologically, much less economically, to care for their loved ones.

Social service agencies and members of churches, synagogues and mosques take responsibility for visiting the sick and helping out with health care issues. But it is our government's responsibility, via a universal health care plan, to see to the health care needs of all people; this includes caregivers of the elderly and disabled.

If it takes a village, including doctors, nurses, teachers and others to care for a child—and it does—and doctors, nurses, technicians and others to care for the sick—and it does—certainly it takes the same amount of human sweat, and more, to care for someone suffering from Alzheimer's or any of the other forms of dementia. I do not know why that daughter killed her mother and then herself. I do know that she was a caregiver who needed help and that her village was not big enough.

September 17, 2007

Oh Good

On a day I don't go there
I call instead.
He says
and he says in perfect English:
I wish this wouldn't have happened to me.
"I know," I say. "I wish it wouldn't have happened to you too."
Thank you, he says.
I'm proud of you, the way you're handling this, I tell him.
Thank you, Sweetheart. I love you. Thank you, he says.
I'll see you tomorrow, I tell him.
Oh, good, he says. *Oh good,*
and the phone is dead.

November 5, 2007

Referring to the disappearance of ego and the desire for knowledge to show off, Thomas Merton writes that "One cannot begin to be an artist. . . until he has become 'empty,' until he has disappeared." In this sense, Abe is becoming a true artist. Perhaps Alzheimer's is one route to Essence. Crap.

November, 2007, Thanksgiving

I'm starting a blog. The *Seattle Post-Intelligencer* online wants it for its online site. Maybe my scribblings about Alzheimer's will help others, even as much as they help me. It's the least I can do this Thanksgiving.

2008

February 16, 2008

It's holy
space
where I come
to be
alone
with poem
and story.

Mind needs
room
free
of past restraints
and habit.

Once reshaped,
mind—

breathing of its own accord
body loosened of now—

becomes
a place
to think
on its
own
volition.

May 23, 2008

Alzheimer's Diary: Wish List

I wish I'd stop holding on
to every little piece of us.
I wish I'd stop making him a saint.
I wish I'd gone on the doctor's trip to Vietnam with him.
I wish his silences wouldn't have bothered me.
I wish Alzheimer's wouldn't exist
but then he wouldn't be here
and he's still him,
really, he is.

June 3, 2008

Us

Once,
before Aphasia ruined his speech,
he said he was glad for all of it,
that I kept him on his toes,
really.

November 25, 2008

Email from Assisted Living Facility nurse

"Abe was found on the floor by his bed on his knees at 9:11 pm last night. His knees looked fine and there appear to be no injuries. The bed alarm went off.

Hope you are enjoying your vacation.

S –"

November 28, 2008

Thanksgiving

Abe has been in a facility for twenty-seven months. He did not drive for two years before that, and, yet, here I am Thanksgiving Day 2008 waiting for him to run to the store to pick up last minute extras.

The kids are here. I play with the grandkids and listen to my adult children coordinate activities for the rest of their vacations. This one's going to the parade, that one to see a friend, and so on. They're lovely, all of them; yet, I walk around with a claw in my chest. Its name is Alzheimer's.

I saw Abe yesterday. For an Alzheimer patient, he was in fine shape. His clothes were clean, his hair was combed and, best of all, he was happy. As soon as he saw me, he smiled his old smile and said, *Well, look who's here*. I sat down next to him and fell in love again.

My husband and I have been living with Alzheimer's for more years than we know, probably ten. He was diagnosed in 2003. I read everything I can get my hands on. I have been a part of four different support groups sponsored by the Alzheimer's Association, including its online community. I now attend a caregivers group at my synagogue.

There is no getting over Alzheimer's. No moving on. Each of us who cares for a person with Alzheimer's has to find ways to cope; these are unique to the individual. Whether the loved one is at home or in a nursing facility, caregiving does not end. It becomes part of the self.

Abe is still Abe. His hands are as warm now as they were when I met him nearly three decades ago. His eyes still twinkle. But he is disconnecting, and my heart breaks every day. All the while I learn more about myself and our relationship—how it is and how it used to be.

I cannot ask him to go to the grocery store. He cannot share holiday dinners with me and the kids. But I have him here. He still teaches me, and for that I am most grateful.

December 1, 2008

Sometimes I think I am living in two different worlds. I guess I am. One is ordinary life, the other is Alzheimer's. In the ordinary world, I play with the dog, read the newspaper, watch our President-Elect work at constructing new paths for a global community, sit at my desk and fill blank sheets of paper with words and sentences I then reorganize. Go to the library to research a book project, talk on the phone with kids and friends, teach a class, and so on.

In the other world, that parallel universe, where some people no longer know their names or their children's faces or the difference between a domino and a cookie, I also take my dog. But here inside the facility Emma does not romp and play. Here she goes from wheelchair to wheel chair to check out smells and attitudes so she can decide whose hand to kiss or face to lick. We find Abe, sit down next to him and wait to see what the day's visit will bring.

There was a time in the last two years when I could bring a newspaper with me, go over a picture story with him and watch him follow along as I read, he reading a word here, a word there. Even now, with aphasia (the inability to access and bring forth language) coupled with the effects of psychotropic drugs, Abe is able to sing a few words of the *Sh'ma Yisrael,* a Hebrew prayer he learned before he was two. But for the most part, we meet on an emotional level with his acceptance and my fear.

I am always afraid. Always. Even with my German Shepherd by my side and the wonderful Foss nursing home staff and the amazingly in touch Group Health hospice team, life makes me afraid, whether in the ordinary world or this, the other, the Alzheimer's world.

Not that there isn't enough religion to back me up. With crosses on the nursing home walls and a *mezuzah* on Abe's door, a Lutheran chaplain at his desk or behind his guitar, a Jewish chaplain always at the ready, not to mention my own rabbi who gives me the 27th psalm to carry in my pocket, and all the other rabbis, teachers and books I seek out for answers, I am more afraid than Abe is (I think).

Alzheimer's makes me shake, but it also provides me with boundaries and for this I am thankful.

What do I mean Alzheimer's provides me with boundaries? Well, it seems to center me. I know this is a paradox. On the one hand Alzheimer's disassembles me; on the other, it forces me to see what I am capable of accomplishing in a twenty-four hour day. It teaches me to whittle, trim, shape and form myself into the person I, alone, am and not the one I needed to be.

December 2, 2008

Just that short time ago we had a whole conversation. They could put him on the phone with me and we could connect. Doesn't matter that I sobbed afterwards, we connected, and he went back to learning how to live his new life, in his new self.

Yesterday when I sat down next to him, I drank coffee and watched him sleep. Then I kissed him and went home. There is no calling anymore. Or sobbing.

later, same day

he doesn't know his favorite elementary teacher was Mrs. Oster
or that he was held back in kindergarten

because he had rheumatic fever
and was mad at his mother
brother
father
without memory his anger is gone
and what he lives for now
is a smile
on anyone's
face

December 4, 2008

The Alzheimer's Association is an important resource for anyone who has questions about Alzheimer's, Alzheimer's caregiving, and the progression of the disease. But I was so caught up in following their Seven Stages of Alzheimer's that may or may not define a victim's place on the continuum, that Abe's doctor looked at me and said, "I don't talk in stages." He was right.

Categorizing disease in stages is important for researchers and for us, as consumers, to be aware of, but they don't tell us everything we need to know about the individual sufferer's (or the caregiver's) precise condition or state of mind.

I see now that the Seven Stages, though helpful, tell me less about the progression of Abe's wanderings through Alzheimer Country than my diaries do.

December 7, 2008

I visit while he sleeps, the Validation Theory, and some thoughts on Asian poetry

Sometimes when I arrive, like today, he's sleeping in our loveseat (the one I brought from home). I kiss his forehead and wait for him to awaken, but he continues his sleep. I sit down next to him and take out my notebook and pen. Maybe I'll get my diary entry done for the day.

Emma, who has accompanied me, watches us. Disappointed that she won't get a pat from the man sitting next to me she sprawls out on the floor and pretends to sleep. Soon a knock on the door rouses her.

One of the care workers wants to know if I'd like a cup of coffee. "It'll keep you company while he sleeps," she says. They're so nice here, and there's a peacefulness that allows for the rest Abe obviously needs.

There's also respect for the individual patient's need for difference in scheduling. Never mind, the staff is on its own schedule. If Abe's not awake in time for breakfast, they let him sleep. If he doesn't want lunch or supper (he still does) they hold his meal and heat it up later.

I don't know if Naomi Feil's Validation Theory is used in training sessions here at Foss Nursing Home and Village, but gentle care as he receives is something I have always looked for when witnessing the goings on at nursing facilities.

Soon, the care worker knocks again. Neither Emma nor Abe budge. With gratitude, I accept a cookie along with the coffee. I'm as grateful for the aide's act of kindness as I am the snack.

I put my notebook and pen down and open the book I had planned to read to Abe today. It's called *Sunset in a Spider Web: Sijo Poetry of Ancient Korea.*

Abe likes to hear me read poems. They are like prayers, and he and prayer have always been close. I especially like the spare *Sijo* form. It's slightly longer than haiku and just as beautiful, just as filled with rosebuds and other smells a brain-disabled person might remember. I recommend these Asian forms for Alzheimer patients.

Though sometimes I read to Abe as he sleeps, I don't feel like it today. I collect Emma, kiss Abe goodbye, and for a few long minutes I stand at the door watching my husband sleep.

As Emma and I walk down the hall, as I say hello to the patients and other family members, as Emma licks this hand and that, I find myself loosening up, feeling relaxed and pleased that Abe was sleeping today. I read by his side, as I used to. It was almost like home.

December 11, 2008

Loveseat

When Abe went into an assisted living facility, on August 17, 2006, I brought our loveseat with us. When he went to the nursing home in January 2007, the loveseat came too. Whatever our relationship had been over the years, our cuddling-selves remained. The staff called us "lovebirds."

As the Alzheimer's progresses my husband is less able to sit, stand or walk. But sometimes he'll find his way to the loveseat and fall asleep there. Then he won't be able to get up or he'll roll onto the floor. Staff advises me to remove the loveseat. I do, and replace it with a lift chair.

I think part of me walks around with blinders on, refusing to acknowledge Alzheimer's presence. Still believing or wishing Abe were healthy and strong.

I try to stay in his moment, in his reality, but I don't move fast enough. I'm the turtle and he's the hare. Am I still waiting for him to get better?

Maybe, but I give the loveseat away.

December 15, 2008

A Question of Language

I have a question about terminology used with Alzheimer's patients:

When Abe can't get up from a chair or stand when he's asked, when he can't sit because his mind no longer tells his body what to do, when he doesn't swallow his medicine because he's forgotten how, why do charts report: Patient refused?

The word "refuse" connotes an ability to decide, an ability and determination to make a decision. If an Alzheimer's patient no longer has this ability, why use language that inadequately reflects the particular circumstance?

This is what I'm Reading

- *The Forgetting: Alzheimer's:, Portrait of an Epidemic* by David Shenk (Anchor paperback, 2003)
- *Dancing with Rose: Finding Life in the Land of Alzheimer's* by Lauren Kessler (Viking, 2007)

December 15, 2008

Same Day 31 degrees outside, unusual for Seattle
Listening to Gershwin

I arrived at the home today around 3. When I went into Abe's room, he was sitting on the edge of the bed. He was agitated and pulling at his clothes. I sat down next to him.

He put his head on my shoulder and said, *Ohh, I love you.* He tried to take his shirt off, but I said: Let's keep it on, and he agreed.

I rubbed his neck and his back for a while and he settled down, mumbling something about the military.

He let me pick up his feet.
His legs were stiff. He couldn't bend them.

I lay him on top of the covers and fixed the pillows under his head.

I put some Gershwin on and after a few minutes of *Swanee,* he fell asleep. I sat with him through *I Got Plenty O Nothin', Somebody Loves Me* and *I Got Rhythm.*

Then I touched base with the nursing team, drove home and came here to my computer to touch base with you.

Tonight I'll find some poetry to read. It relaxes me.

December 16, 2008

If I were a more God-engrossed person, I might be yelling at Him/Her for creating Alzheimer's but since I'm a more science-engrossed person (most of the time), I look to research to find answers to what I don't know. At the same time, I'm amazed at how much *shul* comforts me, even though I don't necessarily believe in the efficacy of prayer. Go figure!

This is what I'm Reading:

- *Learning to Speak Alzheimer's* by Joanne Koenig Coste (Houghton Mifflin, 2003)
- *Talking to Alzheimer's: Simple Ways to Connect When You Visit with a Family Member or Friend* by Claudia J. Strauss (New Harbinger, 2001)
- *The Chassidic Approach to Joy* by Rabbi Shloma Majeski (Sichos in English, 5757-1996)

December 17, 2008

Peter Falk, Hip Surgery & Alzheimer's Disease

I'm as sorry as anyone to read that Peter Falk has fallen victim to Alzheimer's disease. I'm especially interested in his case because the Alzheimer's announcement came with the report that *he recently had hip surgery and required constant care.*

My husband's Alzheimer's diagnosis came after a hip replacement surgery from which he never recovered.

One of the first questions I asked Abe's doctors when I learned that he had Alzheimer's was: *Could there be a causal relationship between hip surgery and the onset of Alzheimer's?* The answer I received, in so many words, was No Chance. I never believed that answer. Not that I thought the doctors weren't telling the truth. I thought they didn't know.

I didn't pursue this at the time but at some point I posed the same question in an Alzheimer's Association online group. A woman responded that her mother also had hip surgery before the Alzheimer's set in. Another coincidence? I wondered.

When I read that Peter Falk had Alzheimer's and recently had hip surgery, I googled: "relationship between hip surgery and Alzheimer's."

Here is the response from a medical text entitled *Hip Surgery: Materials and Developments* edited by Laurent Sedel and Miguel E. Cabanela, published in the United Kingdom by Martin Dunitz (The Livery House)1998.

"The presence of aluminum rich and magnesium-poor neurofibrillar tangles in the cerebral cortex of individuals with Alzheimer's suggests a possible causal relationship between aluminum exposure and this condition." (p. 355) http://www.alz.org/alzwa/documents/alzwa_resource_ad_fs_aluminum.pdf

Here is the Alzheimer's Association's Fact Sheet on Alzheimer's and Aluminum. And another view.

Whatever the view, I'd like to know how much aluminum and other metals were in Abe's hip replacement. I'd like to know if Peter Falk's hip surgery was for a hip replacement and, if so, what the metallic composition of that replacement was. Have any of your loved ones had hip replacement surgeries prior to an Alzheimer's diagnosis? These questions may not help Abe or Peter Falk but, perhaps, they will help others.

This is what I'm reading

- *Walking One Another Home: Moments of Grace and Possibility in the Midst of Alzheimer's* by Rita Bresnahan (Liguori/Triumph, 2003)
- *A Three Dog Life* by Abigail Thomas (Harcourt, 2006)

December 19, 2008

Letter from a Reader

A reader emailed to ask if she should write about her mother's blindness. My first response, after *Thank you for writing*, was—If you're wondering if you should write, you should probably write. This doesn't mean you have to write something good or for publication. Write for yourself. To get the ickiness out, the emotion, good or bad. Certainly if writing makes you feel better, write.

Keep in mind that writing can keep you too much to yourself and sometimes it's better to take a walk than to pick up a pen. But if you're like me you may have to write whether it's good for you or not. I keep a journal. I put everything in it: scribblings, letters I write and don't send, notes about the books I'm reading, photos, doodlings, and so on. But when I write about Alzheimer's, and I need to, perhaps in the same way the reader whose mother is blind needs to, I write specifically about Alzheimer's.

At times, I clump my writings about Alzheimer's in with my ordinary everyday journal, but most of the time I like to keep that subject separate from other things I may be working on, which is why I started this blog. It helps me focus on what I need to learn and say about the disease.

This is what I'm reading:

- *Illness and the Art of Creative Self-Expression* by John Graham-Pole, M.D. (New Harbinger, 2000)
- *Writing as a Way of Healing* by Louise A. DeSalvo (Beacon Press, 2000)

December 23, 2008

Seattle's Snow Days

When I sat down to write this morning, I was thinking how lucky I was to have seen Abe at all this week, what with the ice and snow blocking my door. Thanks to my cousin Leonid's four-wheel drive, we made it out of my driveway, off my street and northwest to Foss.

About ten days ago, Abe's condition worsened and once the snow started falling, I worried about getting to see him. He could barely stand up, and when he did, he veered to the left.

I thought he had a mini-stroke and said to him: "I think you might have had a little stroke."

Maybe I did and maybe I didn't! Abe snapped. With a Yiddish shrug. And without a trace of aphasia interrupting his speech.

One minute I think we're losing him, the next he's on top of his game.

"You must be exhausted," someone said to me the other day.

I am. But I can't imagine how exhausted Abe must be. Or the members of the nursing home staff who make it in. They're the ones who deserve the gold medal.

This is what I'm reading:

- *Proust and the Squid: The Story and Science of the Reading Brain* by Maryanne Wolf (Harper, 2007)
- *The Healing Art: A Doctor's Black Bag of Poetry* by Rafael Campo (Norton, 2003)
- *Regarding the Pain of Others* by Susan Sontag (Farrar, Straus and Giroux, 2003)

December 26, 2008

Unsuccessful Visit

My visit with Abe yesterday wasn't as successful as my visits are on most days. As I walked in I could see that he was engrossed in picking at the Alert Device wrapped around the chair next to him, trying to understand it I think.

Instead of waiting until he was finished (I knew it could take an hour) after I said "Hi," I asked him if I could put the device (I forget what it's called) on the table. He said: *No.*

I started to pull the chair out to sit on. He became upset, didn't know who was talking to him (though a familiar twinkle began to emerge, then waned). When I tried to touch him he swiped me away, said: *Don't touch me.*

I don't know what I was thinking. Or not thinking.

I didn't have to visit him yesterday, but it was Christmas and I thought there would be too much stimulation for him, too many people mulling around, and he'd become upset. And I had made such an effort to get there. Once again, my cousin and his four-wheel drive picked me up and made it through the snow.

Abe did not need me or our cousin to visit, to hover over him while he was engrossed in something we weren't connected with. I needed to be with Abe, he did not need to be with me.

My son, Ian says: "Mom, You don't have to be there every day for him to know he's loved."

As it was, the place was peaceful, well-managed, quiet. Staff were in touch with the needs of the residents, most of whom were watching Pavarotti. Their only annoyances (as I could see) came from an occasional visitor, me included. (This doesn't mean residents shouldn't have visitors but that we might be better visitors. At least, I might).

I'm having trouble understanding what my role is now that Abe's cognition and physical condition have declined so. He doesn't need me as much as he used to, even as much as a few weeks ago. My job is to check his environment, to see that he's okay, that he's well-taken care of. It's to be cognizant of his reality (in as much as that's possible), and it's to be cognizant of my own.

What should I have done when I first walked in and saw that my visit was an intrusion. Sit there, watch him, then leave? Wait around? Go to the library across the street? Then come back? Maybe so.

This is what I'm reading:

- *Elegy for Iris* by John Bayley (St. Martin's Press, 1999)
- *Grief* by Andrew Holleran (Hyperion, 2006)

December 30, 2008

A word like 'schedule'

Every day is different. Some days he wakes up early the next day, noon. A word like "schedule" has no meaning. Nor does "menu." He eats less now. Some days only fifty percent. In the afternoon, I'm scared. At night, more so. But tomorrow I can hold his hand. Or maybe I just won't go.

This is what I'm reading:

- *The Beauty of the Husband: A Fictional Essay in 29 Tangos* by Anne Carson (Alfred A. Knopf, 2001)
- *The Story of My Father: A Memoir* by Sue Miller (Random House Trade Paperbacks, 2003)

2009

January 1, 2009

Fragments from an Alzheimer's Journey

1

He's Sadness
and thin,
scared,
confused—
a bird looking for its mother.
There is no pill for this
not for him,
not for me
I give him a pear.
He eats it all—
bit by bit
until
it's
gone.

2

Today I wheel him
to the window
where he points outside
and says:
He's dying
I say:
Who's dying?
He says:
That guy

3

More and more
he slips into himself
unwaiting for me to join him.
A man, still. The same face
hardly changed.
But for cognition and the lack
of affect
who would know
he won't remember us—
when I leave.

4

His face is our grandfather's
staring out from an old picture frame
a reminder that love is like the moon
waning into different shapes—
crescents, slits

5

Today when I walked into his room he was sitting in the wheelchair staring. His eyes were red, and I thought he had been crying, but there were no tears. He didn't know me. I looked straight into him and said:

"Hi Abe. I'm Esther. I'm your wife.

I'm Esther."

Really?

"Really," I said.

And he was alive again.

6

He's better today,
recognized me when I came in
took my hand and kissed it.

Later, he kissed his own hand.

He has a bruise,
and he kissed the bruise
as if he were a father caring for a child,
something like the day
he called himself *He.*

7

Tonight at Dinner

A dish of pears
6 ounces of health shake
4 ounces of apple juice
The rest: spit out.
Chewing's hard.
Swallowing
liquid's easier.
To myself, I think:
I'm tired,
I want to go home.
But where is home?
Here, at the nursing
home or in that other place
where we used to live?

8

HE'S BEDRIDDEN
bedridden
bedridde
bedridd
bedrid
bedri
bedr
bed
be
b

9

He's weak and tired
his hands curl into fists
they're cold and clammy
his arms are cool
the rest of him is warm

he opens his eyes and says: *We did it*
then falls back to sleep

10

How long
can a body do this?

Whose body am I talking
about anyway,

mine or his?

I'm not sure
I know
the difference.

11

Neither pear nor peach satisfy him.
He barely drinks the shake
and doesn't understand the word, *cookie*.

But he smiles and holds my hand. He calls me *Hon*.
When I leave, I kiss him and say: "Goodbye." Again.

12

Again.

January 4, 2009

Mostly, we look through *National Geographic* or *Sunset Magazine*

He can't stand by himself anymore. He needs at least two people, one with a safety belt, to help him out of a chair. The walker takes him only so far, then he needs a wheelchair—although yesterday when I arrived, he was walking with the walker back and forth down the hall. I think maybe sometimes he knows how to walk and at other times he doesn't. The same for sitting up.

He eats less because he can't chew or has forgotten how. Swallowing is no longer automatic. He's lost 12 pounds in six weeks. Starting today, we're trying pureed food.

People ask if he knows who I am. Sometimes he won't let anyone care for him until I get there so, yes, I think he does.

I don't read to him much anymore because it's hard to get him up from sitting in the community room to take him into his room where we can sit quietly. I usually take out a puzzle and start doing it, maybe he'll follow. Or I find crayons. Mostly, we look through *National Geographic* or *Sunset Magazine*. He reads a word here, a word there.

He still accesses language—medical terms, even whole sentences. The other day, he asked a nurse how her lymph nodes were. At dinner last night, he made lines on a napkin with an eating utensil. I asked him if he was doing an autopsy. His eyes lit up and he said: *Yes.*

This is what I'm reading:

- *Musicophilia: Tales of Music and the Brain* by Oliver Sacks (Vintage, 2007)

January 6, 2009

From Abe's perspective

There's still this one woman who kisses me goodbye. Her name seems to be Esther and she comes to see me a lot. Sometimes I see worry in her face or tears in her eyes. But sometimes she laughs at just the right places. Like yesterday at dinner when I didn't want to eat and did the frozen section. She knew exactly what I was doing. I don't know how she knew, but she knew.

I unfolded a napkin and with a much-too-dull knife, I drew three straight lines. Well, of course, they were straight. Perfectly straight, the way I always drew lines. Then when I was making the usual incisions into the tissue, the woman, Esther, got excited. She asked me: "Are you doing a frozen section?"

Why yes, I said, and her eyes lit up as if a miracle just happened. And perhaps it did. (Actually I was doing an autopsy, but she got confused).

It is strange, isn't it, that I can remember how to do a frozen section when I don't remember what a frozen section is. The brain is funny that way. There's so much we don't understand, but there is hope.

Miracles like "the frozen section incident" happen all the time. Even with people who appear to have lost all memory. One merely has to listen and watch. Watch closely. This disease I have, this Alzheimer's, which invaded my mind without my permission, opens up possibilities for a whole new frontier of knowledge.

Tragic as it is for AD victims and for family and friends who share in the experience, Alzheimer's disease contributes to an understanding of the human condition. It helps us learn, not only about people who have the disease but about those in the surrounding social, economic and political world, as well as about those in the medical and scientific worlds.

January 12, 2009

A twinkle in his eye

There was no twinkle in Abe's eye yesterday, not much the day before either. Today I brought him sorbet and a banana. He ate the banana but not the sorbet. I gave the sorbet to Emma, then she kissed the residents who like her. She annoys Abe now, so stays out of his way.

Abe peeled the banana himself, not a small thing. Sometimes he can't open it. Why he could today, I don't know, but when I turned my head away from Emma to help him peel the banana, it was already peeled.

After he ate the banana, he went back to picking at his pant leg. He was doing that when I came in. I asked him what he was doing. Did he want to take his pants off? Was something annoying him? I wanted to help, but he was focused and not about to let anyone in.

Emma and I sat with him for half an hour. When we left he was still engrossed in his pant leg. He wasn't interested in kissing me goodbye.

Afterwards I went to my cousins' for dinner. It was nice, the six of us. We hardly mentioned Abe, but there he was smiling, a twinkle in his eye.

January 14, 2009

Today I went at 3 pm and what a difference. The visit was bookended by two smiles, the first when I walked in. He recognized me immediately and his smile reached across his face. The nurse's aide said, "Look he recognizes you." She was as happy as Abe and I were.

At the end of my visit, as I was walking toward the door, he smiled and waved a gentle fist goodbye. (He couldn't open his hand. I'm not sure why.) In between the smiles was more confusion, though less than last night.

January 16, 2009

Email to the kids

. . . Last night it looked to me and the staff as if Abe didn't have much time left. He was comfortable but very weak . . . mom

January 17, 2009

He was

            better today
recognized me when I came in
took my hand and kissed it.
Ate a cup of ice cream, strawberry
with medicine in it
and 3 to 4 ounces of health shake.

A few days ago
I didn't think I'd make it to the opera tomorrow.
I thought I'd be arranging a funeral
but I'll go to the opera
and out to eat with a friend.
I'll pretend the day is "normal."
Maybe it is.

January 23, 2009

Can't ambulate

He's in a wheelchair now, can't help get himself out of it, and he's too heavy to lift. So the staff borrows a mechanical lift from another unit to get him up.

The care at Foss has been good, more than good. But just when I'm thinking I hope they don't have to move him to another unit, the head nurse calls to tell me they may have to move him to another unit. She says I'll be able to check out the new room first.

Maybe it won't happen, but if it does, I hope the new staff will be as kind to Abe—and to me—as this group of people have been. And I hope Obama's team increases the minimum wage and nursing home aides' salaries!

January 26, 2009

A complaining day

Today was the pits. Did absolutely nothing. Got no work done. No play done. Not even the dog park, though I did talk to a friend and a couple of the kids.

The only way I could center myself was to sleep before and after the nursing home. Even there, I slept in the electric lift chair, the one he didn't need, after all. Remember the lift chair, the one that replaced the loveseat?

I did socialize a bit in the nursing home, wrote in my journal, talked to some residents, family members and staff. One resident who grew up with German Shepherds took Emma's leash. The woman was happy, and that was fun to see.

Still, the nursing home, particularly the Alzheimer's unit, is a different world, a parallel universe, as I've said, where every day is different. Difference in every eight-hour shift. Even hour to hour, minute to minute: change.

Today, this afternoon, Abe's sleeping. Now he's alert. Either way, he doesn't know me. Though he's pleasant enough. (This isn't about you, Esther).

I feed him a cup of custard. I'm afraid it'll stick in his throat, but it doesn't. He loves it. Maybe swallowing's easier when lying down.

The nurse comes in: Abe smiles. The nurse's assistant comes in: Abe says: *There you are*, as if she's his best friend. I'm jealous. I can't believe I'm jealous. Imagine! What kind of sense does that make. Jealousy is one emotion we don't need here in this alien country of unremembered lives.

But it raises the question: Is it ok for me to kiss him goodbye? I mean, if he doesn't know who I am? Wouldn't it seem funny to be kissed on the lips by a stranger?

I kiss him anyway. Maybe he'll remember me tomorrow. Either way, I'm out the door. I know it's time for another life, but I'm not in the mood to get one.

I suppose I did do something today. I helped in the nursing home and came closer to understanding what goodbye means.

I'll get something done in my other world, the one where I read books, go to movies and write, soon enough. And then, no doubt, I'll complain of wanting the other world back, the one where Abe doesn't remember but is.

January 29, 2009

Abe didn't look well this evening, and I had another one of those: "Is he going to live through the night" feelings. But he held onto my hand as if he knew me.

He was in the wheelchair and when he fell asleep for the second or third time, I cut his mustache and what I could of his beard, and when the nurse's aide came to get him for bed and I told him goodnight, he said goodnight back.

The aide said: "Did you hear? He said goodnight back," and before I could get out the door, she hugged me. The nurse, did too. He thanked me for the tulips and for brightening the night. I didn't know I did that. I thought I was just going to see Abe.

February 3, 2009

Watch yourself, Esther

In witnessing Alzheimer's I have to observe my own health and behavior as well as my husband's. From my mood of the last few days I see that it's time to move on, even in small ways. I've disliked the expression "move on" when I've heard it, when well-meaning people suggest I turn away from Alzheimer's and climb a mountain, say, or go Salsa dancing or party until three in the morning.

First of all, I'm not in the habit of doing any of those things so I'm not going to accept the suggestion to do one of them now. "That's exactly what you should do", Person A says, "Something utterly new." Well, utterly or not, I'm not about to start climbing mountains today. But I do love movies. That's one thing Abe and I did together a lot. We held hands, ate popcorn, held hands, ate popcorn, held hands and watched the figures on the screen pass by.

So today I take up movies again. I'm going to become a serious movie watcher, not just old movies on Turner Classics, though I adore that channel, but out-in-the-world movies, in theatres where hubs of people join together to be entertained.

I have a movie buddy, a special friend who cared for her husband at home for four years. I've known Millie for maybe thirty years, but only since our husbands' illnesses have we become real friends. I can say to her: "I want him to die already (toi toi) or I don't ever want to go to that nursing home again or I just want to jump off the face of the earth." And she can say whatever she wants to me.

I'm also sick of reading books on Alzheimer's. February is Black History month and I've started this week's reading with the late Seattle-based writer Octavia E. Butler's *Parable of the Sower*. Butler (1947-2006) was the *first black woman to gain national prominence as a science fiction writer*. I'm going to enjoy her work and, for me, a new genre.

Then I'll go to the nursing home to make sure Abe gets some liquid in him. I'll kiss him hello, hold his hand, and then I'll kiss him good-bye. Again.

February 4, 2009

This and That

When I went to see Abe yesterday around 4, he was in bed. His head was stuck in a t-shirt he was trying to remove. I fixed the t-shirt, rearranged the pillow under his head, and sat and watched him until he fell asleep.

Then, as I told myself I would, I went with a friend to the movies.

Later, I read some of Susan Sontag's early diaries and more of Octavia E. Butler's *Parable*.

I didn't empty the dishwasher and did nothing about the pile of dishes in the sink.

I talked to a few of the kids, walked the dog, listened to CNN, did Facebook (which makes me laugh), turned on the fireplace and went to bed. I didn't call the nursing home.

Later I woke up to remember the Activities Director telling me that a classical pianist came to play at the home the other day. Abe and his wheelchair were next to the piano. She said he was all smiles. That afternoon, he played ball.

February 5, 2009

I curl up in his lift chair, Emma at my feet

I walk into Abe's room. He's sleeping or, at least, his eyes are closed. While Emma settles at my feet, I curl up in the lift chair Abe no longer uses and close my eyes. The pump attached to the end of the new inflatable bed makes so much noise I can't hear myself think. Nor can I hear him breathe. I get up to check. His eyes are open. He's staring into Nothing.

I touch his shoulder, call his name; he looks at me without affect. His smile is gone. I know that the smile is one of those manifestations of emotion that Alzheimer's patients lose in this last stage, but every time I see the downturn of his mouth, I think he's crying (tears or not).

I don't know what to do so I sit on the edge of the bed and sing the *sh'ma*, which turns out to be as close to an our song as we've ever had. He turns his head and looks at me with the same intensity that he used to look into Nothing. I've grabbed his attention! He's with me.

I sing the *sh'ma* again and the corners of his mouth turn up. All of a sudden, in a distinct and rather loud voice, he says: *God, God, I will look for* . . . He looks at me and I sing the *sh'ma* for a third time. He says in a voice softer than before: *I need* . . . and falls into sleep.

In a few minutes he awakens and I feed him keylime pie yogurt. Key-lime pie was his favorite dessert. Yogurt is as close as I can get to something he may be able to swallow. He opens his mouth and, like a bird, takes what I give him until three quarters of the yogurt is gone.

It's 5 p.m. now. The nurse's aides come in with the Vanderlift to get him dressed, out of bed, and into the wheelchair. Dinner will be in an hour. I don't stay. I don't have the patience to stay. I kiss him good-bye. It doesn't matter if he knows who I am. We engaged each other. One person to another. Doesn't matter who we were, or are.

February 6, 2009

I'm smiling. . . in the face of his dying. . . he would be smiling too, if he could.

He would love that I can do this much on the computer. He retired around the time he had to start using one. He was happy with the card catalog and index cards. I love them too, just to flip through.

Time to go see how he's doing. The nurse said he smiled this morning and had some liquid. I'll bring some jello and see what's what.

February 10, 2009

Barry Levinson

I watched *Avalon* today, spent 2+ hours outside the world of Alzheimer's and inside the world I grew up in, Barry Levinson's Baltimore. I couldn't wait to see the movie when it came out in 1990. I thought it was going to be about the Avalon Movie Theatre on Park Heights Ave. Here is where I spent whole days watching cowboy Westerns. In the 1950s and earlier, a kid could stay in a movie house all day, watching and rewatching the same Western or short or newsreel or Bugs Bunny cartoon. Which I did.

Hours and hours with or without friends or siblings. Even on Pesach/Passover, I came with my matzo and schmaltz sandwiches to watch Roy Rogers, Dale Evans, Gene Autry, Tex Ritter (John's father) and the damsels in distress they rescued from Blackie's clutches which led me straight to Jane Eyre, Mr. Rochester and an ideology of rescuing the oppressor.

Levinson's *Avalon* wasn't about my precious movie house with the ripped screen and screaming kids but I loved the movie anyway. Barry's *Avalon*, about the growth of the city, immigration and the move to the suburbs, brought me back to East Baltimore's marble steps and Park Heights Ave's row houses.

I'm glad I took in the movie (on the Indieplex channel 513 in Seattle). It gave me time to recoup before the onslaught of the next phase of the AD process. For no sooner do I turn off the TV than I get a call from the nursing home: they're moving Abe to another unit. He needs an environment where Vanderlifts are indigenous. Who knew?

February 11, 2009

They're moving Abe to another unit Friday. Since he can no longer walk, it's not necessary for him to be in an Alzheimer's unit.

February 19, 2009

Lack
for Ian who noticed

I never saw his face
like that

strings of blue—
veins—

where beard
had been

so pink and new
like baby skin

I never saw his face
like that

so soft and trim
a lack

like that.

I never saw
Abe's face
like that.

February 22, 2009

A dozen damn donuts

I sit by his bed. It's 3:30 p.m. He's sleeping. I watch him for only a few minutes, then tell the aide: "I'll be back." But I don't go back. I leave the nursing home thinking I'll go back/knowing I won't.

Instead, I get in the car and go to Krispy Kreme Doughnuts. I never go to Krispy Kreme Doughnuts. I don't buy donuts. I don't eat donuts. I live across the street from Top Pot Donuts and I don't even go in there because I don't buy donuts. I mean never. When did you ever see me buy a donut?

But on this day, for some reason, for some I'm-gonna-eat-a-donut reason, I buy a whole dozen darn donuts. Not only that, I sit in the car and eat three of them. Even let my dog watch. (They're all chocolate so I can't give her one.) When did I ever eat three donuts? Never. I mean, they're not my favorite form of self-destruction.

So I'm at that point, am I? Everybody told me what happens to caregivers. In one way or another, they self-destruct. Well, I won't. Tomorrow, I go to the Y. Or Curves.

Have I mentioned that I dislike gyms almost as much as I dislike malls? Well, tomorrow I go to the gym even before I go to the nursing home. And maybe I won't go to the nursing home tomorrow. Or the next day. That's probably a lie, but at least, I'll change my schedule. I usually write in the morning. I'll go to the gym instead.

At one point, I thought if Abe died and I stopped going, I'd miss the home. I'd miss the other residents, the staff and the families I've gotten to know. But since he's moved upstairs, I don't feel that way. This is Abe's last stop, and whether he knows it or not, for me, it's just too much.

Tomorrow I'll join the Y. I think I'll like that best. For one, it's in the University District, near me, and 1 can get a personal trainer there. I hear that's the going thing. The thought of going to a gym and getting a PT nauseates me, but not half as much as those donuts did.

February 25, 2009

Ash Wednesday

Visiting Abe tonight had an interesting twist. I came in after he was washed and readied for bed. He looked sweet. His face was pink and beautifully clean. Except . . . the aide must have missed a spot.

When she comes by I mention that Abe has a black smudge on his forehead. I don't know what it is. She leans over him to get a closer look, says: "Oh, it's Ash Wednesday. The minister put ashes on every-body's forehead."

I'm dumfounded, speechless; yet, I'm able to laugh. All of a sudden, I'm able to laugh, and it feels good. I say to the aide "We're Jewish," and she laughs. "I'm Muslim."

I guess it doesn't hurt to cover all the bases, does it?

February 26, 2009

He looked at me with mind

Today when I read from Naomi Shihab Nye's "Envy:"

The white cat
on the white chair
lives white minutes
I'm not even in

He said: *That's beautiful,* and when I started to get up, he said: *Don't go.*

Imagine. Two sentences. And he looked at me—with mind.

The move to the second floor has been good for him. He's more alert and he shows more affect. Today, as people passed us in the hall, he smiled his crinkly-eyed smile and a young blonde visitor caught his eye.

Meanwhile, I joined the Y and Silver Sneakers, had my first exercise class and consultation with the Y's personal trainer, both good experiences. I especially like doing the strengthening stuff and working out with weights. Who knew?

February 28, 2009

Beardless & Ash Wednesday again

He looked so frail tonight, more so than usual. I wish they hadn't shaved his beard off. He looks more like his brother now than he does himself. I don't know why they had to shave his beard off. He's had it over forty years. I wonder how his face feels to him now? Does he know? Does it itch? When he touches his face does he feel something's missing? They shouldn't have cut his beard off. They should have included me in that decision. I don't know why I feel worse about his beard than I do the cross on his forehead on Ash Wednesday, but I do. They had no business shaving him. I've never seen him without a beard except in pictures when he was young, maybe in his thirties and before. He's lost so much weight, forty pounds and he loses more every day. The speech therapist changed his diet from "pureed" to "mechanical soft," also without consulting me. He can't eat that food, can't swallow, keeps it in his cheeks, until it falls out or he figures how to spit it out. He's so thin. It's better if he drinks a health shake, which provides nutrition, than to worry him with food he can't swallow. He's so thin, and now his beard's gone. When I got there at 5:30 tonight, he was in the dining room asleep in his wheelchair. He had a paper cup of something slipping out of his hand and most of what had been in the cup was on his shirt. He wasn't the only one. Everyone was waiting for dinner. He had his red t-shirt on. He looks beautiful in red and with the beard gone his face is all pink like a baby's. I took the cup from his hand and wiped his shirt. He continued sleeping, his mouth open, then closed, then open. I don't know why they had to shave his beard off. I loved his beard. Later in bed he wakened a bit but still I couldn't get him to drink, much less eat. He knew me.

When I said I love you, he said *Me too*, smiled a little, then went back to sleep. The sleep's from not refusing his medicine. I can't stand that they shaved him. The first time I saw him shaved last week, I worried more about his face itching and how it would feel as it grew back than anything else. Everybody said how great he looked and he did look great, but now they did it again and so unexpectedly. "That's what they do with men in the mornings," one nurse told me. Maybe so, but not to men with beards. Darn it. I wonder how he feels when he's being shaved. It's not as if he doesn't have feelings anymore. He's still Abe, and I'm still Esther. I don't know him without a beard. I didn't know he had little veins in his face or that his ears stuck out like that. I didn't know there was all that vulnerability under a beard. I didn't ever know men were so vulnerable as that.

March 1, 2009

Just home from the dog park and a good walk with Emma. Fun
to see her next to a 160 pound St. Bernard. Big as Emma is her 75
pounds could have walked under him.

I had planned to see Abe after the dog park, but all night long I
dreamed of driving to The Home, getting out of the car with a bottle
of water, forgetting the water somewhere, then not being able to find
his room once off the elevator and on the right floor. The dream
goes on and on. I'm back in graduate school, then back, back to years
earlier when my kids were little and old age was something I didn't
know about. Then forward again to I-don't- know-where.

So I didn't go to the Nursing Home. The dream helped me not go. I
went home instead, dried Emma off and came here to decide what
poems I'll read at the reading tonight. I don't know if I'll get to Abe's
today or not.

March 4, 2009

Cheekbones & an elderly stranger

Abe was so beautiful tonight. We've been married 27 years and have known each other 28, but in all that time I don't think I've noticed his cheekbones.

He slept in his wheelchair throughout my visit. I sat on his bed and watched him. He's lost about fifty pounds. His face is thin and sculpted. He is pure Abe, pristine and whole. His cheekbones are stunning.

I'm taken aback. On the one hand, absence of his beard has upset me more than I initially thought it would (I've asked them not to shave him again); on the other hand, the shaven face has allowed me to see newness where I hadn't before. Newness, as in a newborn's newness, absent of scars and blemishes that come with living.

I'm reminded of a night 28 years ago. We weren't yet married. We were in Ravenna, walking down N.E. 65th St. when a man fell in front of a bus. We hurried over. Abe helped the man up as the shaken bus driver jumped out, and I called 911.

The man who fell in the street must have been about the age Abe is now, 80. Later we learned that he had walked out of his nursing home and was trying to get back to his real home in Alaska. He had dementia. His children brought him to Seattle to be near them. He couldn't find his way home because he was looking for the street he used to live on.

The face I watched tonight, the one in the wheelchair, was as beatific as the one I observed 28 years ago. Then Abe was a gentle citizen-doctor looking in the eyes of an elderly stranger, stroking his arm, caring for him until help came. Now he is the elderly stranger, strange to some, perhaps even to himself, but not to me.

March 5, 2009

he's more now
than he was
then,
before
he lost
who he
was—
a new-born
starting
fresh,
the whole
world
ahead of
him
is he really dying
or just be-
coming
something
new?

I'm not at all sure what I mean by any of this. I don't believe in
reincarnation or in those other lives some think we go to or come
from. I think the body goes six feet (or is it four feet nowadays?)
under (if it's not cremated) and if there's a soul, the soul lives in
the consciousness of those who are living. If I were a true-believer,
maybe I'd think the soul goes back to God. But I'm not all that true
of a believer. What I know about God is nothing; if I said anything

different, I'd be presumptuous. What I know of organized religion and tribal communities is that they carry with them an "us and them" mentality (I'm not free of this) that causes more problems than not.

Yet, when I look at the tininess of Abe, the sweetness and what seems like purity from the absence of toxins that too much life brings on, I see a new human being, unprotected yet protected all the while. By what, I don't know, but something in his face, even when filled with discomfort seems to say something else is happening to Abe besides his dwindling away toward nothingness. Something seems to be preserving him. I don't know what it is, but it seems holy.

Do we all wear halos but see them only towards the end?

March 6, 2009

The self is more than ego

Thanks to a reader I met on Facebook I picked up a copy of *Still Alice* this weekend, a gripping read. I couldn't put it down.

For those living through Alzheimer's, whether as caregiver or victim, I understand why they wouldn't want to read one more sentence about Alzheimer's. After years of dealing with the disease and studying this opinion and that, reader's fatigue sets in. But *Still Alice* will pick you up again. It's all about the idea of self and its practical manifestations in everyday life. Though Genova doesn't use these words—the language is mine and she may disagree—for me the characters of Alice and her husband, John, demonstrate firsthand the relationship between ego and self.

Every time I hear someone say "Abe's self is gone," or "He's not Abe" anymore, I cringe. From the beginning and that seems so long ago I can't remember when—7, 8, 9, 10 years—I've said Abe is still Abe. His spirit is still here. He's still with us. Not only does Lisa Genova, author of *Still Alice*, validate my perspective, she helps me see exactly what I mean when I speak about the self in relation to Alzheimer's.

Abe's not interested in showing himself off (not that he was ever a big showoff). He doesn't need to compete. He doesn't need to display competence in his field of study or be present at a meeting or do a good job anywhere. He doesn't need to know what's going on in the news or around the corner. Nor does he need to worry about social or professional consequences, think about making a good impression, not with colleagues, friends or acquaintances.

Sad, yes, of course, tragic. But none of this means that his self is gone or that he's not still here. His self is not just ego; his self has other components as well, including remnants of id and even super-ego. More reason for society to step in and help AD patients.

Through the successes and failures of Alzheimer's learning, Alice and her family develop the capacity to see beyond their personal need to charm or know. Alzheimer's teaches this family that there is more to the self than ego. Even though she is no longer a Harvard professor, Alice is still here. We know this because Lisa Genova, the author and creator of *Still Alice* writes her novel from Alice's point of view. Genova can do this because Alice has Early Onset Alzheimer's —she is only 50 years old—and she knows she has Alzheimer's. She is aware of what's happening to her. I don't know if this is always true but in this particular story it is, and as Genova is a Ph.D. in neuroscience, a strong researcher in close touch with sufferers of Early Onset AD, I trust that Alice's awareness could be authentic.

Abe's case is different. He's eighty, not fifty. Still, I wonder how old he was when he began to develop AD. Genova's novel, backed by her research into Alzheimer's Disease, gives me hope that future generations of victims and caregivers will know what they're in for a lot earlier than Abe and I did.

March 10, 2009

Bluebeard's Castle

Saturday night I went with a friend to see *Bluebeard's Castle*. I don't know much about opera, but I can't imagine another troupe putting on a better rendition of *Bluebeard* or *Erwartung* than the Seattle Opera did. A spectacular evening. Except I wasn't in the right frame of mind to go to the opera or anywhere else. It's true what they say about "the long goodbye." One is forever in a state of mourning, so no matter how stunning the settings, the orchestra, the arias, I am hard-pressed to find joy in a musical night out.

Jewish law instructs the mourner of a primary relative not to listen to music for a year after the death. This guideline—and it's only a guideline—includes not attending musical performances. My husband is still very much alive, but I am in a state of mourning and have been for a long time. I wish the rabbis would create a set of behavior guidelines for Alzheimer spouses so we wouldn't be so confused about what we should be doing in the course of the long dying.

Ok, so I'm a little ticked off. When I came home from the opera, I forgot to set the clock ahead an hour, so Sunday morning I walked into my caregiver's support group an hour late. On the way home I tripped over a curb, banged up my knee, chin, lips and nose, all because my hands were in my pockets as I had forgotten my gloves.

No matter, my kids are two blocks away and always carry emergency kits. We washed me up and took the dogs to the park. Dogs can't wait for faces to heal.

Monday I stayed in bed reading, writing and feeling sorry for myself. Today, even though I was afraid my swollen face would scare him, I went to see Abe. He looked at me as if I were an alien, I mean more so than usual.

Oh well, tomorrow will be better. Emma's barking. I better take her out.

March 15, 2009

Hands

Saturday: Emma and I arrive at 3:45 p.m. Abe's just getting up from his afternoon nap. The lady across the hall is excited to see a dog. She wheels herself over, and Emma gives her a lick.

Inside his room, we watch as the aide prepares Abe for the Vander-lift. She maneuvers him into the sling. He's scared. He grabs onto a part of the lift he's not supposed to touch, but it's the only thing he has to hold onto. I've seen him do this before. It frustrates the aides. I take his hand and say he's scared. She says: "I know."

He doesn't have Alzheimer's. He's alert, alert enough to be scared. How can he be this alert and have Alzheimer's? Maybe he never had it. Maybe he has vascular disease or lewy body or maybe it's a brain tumor.

He knows me. I know he knows me. He holds my eyes through-out the Vanderlift transfer from bed to wheelchair. I ask the aide if we can try to let him walk. No, she says. I must talk to the nurse or physical therapist. She's right, of course. They're well-trained here.

Another aide comes in, a man who looks like he's never seen a dog, much less a German Shepherd. Emma barks. Loud. A German Shepherd loud. I take her downstairs to Abe's old unit to say hello to the residents. Then I take her back to the car, tell her she's a pain, go back upstairs, apologize to the man who's country doesn't love dogs the way America does and continue into Abe's room.

2

I wheel Abe up and down the hall. We stop to talk to a man who also can't talk. These two men, powerful in their day—to me powerful still —say hello to each other with their eyes. After a few minutes, I think they've had enough of one another's discomfort. I don't know why I think this—perhaps it's I who's had enough—and I wheel Abe into a small out-of-the-way room so we can sit by ourselves.

I take out a yellow pad and write ABE on the page. Then draw a picture of a smiley face. I feel stupid. I'm trying too hard. I think he thinks this is stupid, too.

He studies his hands, seems to want to tell me something about his hands. Perhaps he doesn't recognize them. They haven't been this thin since he was a boy. We turn his hands over, trace the lines, turn them over again and retrace. He seems agitated, not a lot, but enough for me to know he's had enough of this activity. So have I. We fold his hands into his lap.

I wheel him into the hall again, pass the man who still can't talk and find the big-screen TV room. There's junk on, but the atmosphere is friendly, like the aides are. I get us coffee and health shake. Soon I don't think he recognizes me anymore.

I show him the book I've been carrying in my bag, *In the Palm of Your Hand* by Steve Kowit (Tilbury House, 1995) . There's an illustration on the front cover of two hands playing the string game, what's it called? The Cat's Cradle. I used to play it as a kid and years later played it with my own kids. Cat's Cradle, never thought to play it with Abe. I'll bring string in next time and see what we can do with it.

He can't possibly have AD. He's studying the book, paging through it in the same way he did his medical journals. High forehead creased in concentration. No one looking at this little man in the wheelchair would think he has Alzheimer's. He shows no frustration. Only I'm frustrated, think I should have set a picture book on the table, but he seems to like the words. After about ten minutes, he gives me the book.

It's dinner time. I wheel him into the dining room. His face looks blank again. Maybe all the while I've thought he's been with me, he hasn't. Maybe I've just been imagining his interest in things, his interest in me. But when I lean down to kiss him goodbye, say: "I'll see you tomorrow," he kisses me back and says:

goo
bye
swee
har

March 20, 2009

I didn't see him

yesterday
or the day before.
I was too burned out.
I went today.
When he saw me,
he said,
You're good
and fell back to sleep.
Then I left.

March 21, 2009

Alzheimer's & Death Instinct

Sigmund Freud wrote that the aim of "life is death," but you couldn't prove that by Abe. Sometimes when I go to see him I do feel as if I'm looking Death in the face; but rest assured, meeting up with cheap Death is not Abe's aim, not by any means. This man is *not going gently into that good night*. This is what I witness. This is what I see.

This is what I'm reading:

- *Do Not Go Gentle Into That Good Night* by Dylan Thomas
- *The Death of Sigmund Freud: The Legacy of His Last Days* by Mark Edmundson (Bloomsbury, 2007)

March 25, 2009

Mr. and Mrs. Canary, Abe's weight and Alice Sebold

Yesterday: I arrive at Abe's at 3:00 pm. He's in the community/dining room listening to one of the staff sing country western.

Abe looks uncomfortable (not due to the music). He seems to recognize me though. I wash his face and hands and he perks up a little. I offer him a health shake; he drinks a full eight ounces.

After awhile, I wheel him around the halls, then we go for a ride on the elevator. In the front lobby are two canaries whom I call Mr. Yellow and Mrs. Blue. Mrs. Blue is shy, but Mr. Yellow makes enough noise to grab Abe's attention.

Then we visit the Alzheimer's unit, Abe's first home at Foss, the secure unit for people who wander. He lights up. The nurse and aides and activity director give him hugs and kisses and he speaks more in these few minutes than he did in the last hour.

I know they had to move him upstairs but the downstairs AD unit had really become home to him. And to me too. Everybody asks for Emma, but I left her home today. I can't deal with her and a man in a wheelchair.

I wheel Abe around to say hello to the other residents, he drinks four ounces of apple juice! Then we say goodbye, see Mr. and Mrs. Canary on the way to the elevator and go back upstairs.

All and all an okay visit, except for his weight. 159 lbs. It wasn't so long ago that he weighed 215 lbs and we didn't know how he was going to lose all that weight. Some things you just shouldn't worry about. I probably won't make it there until 4 today. I'm not even dressed yet, had to finish the book I was reading, Alice Sebold's *The Lovely Bones.*

Why I chose to read *The Lovely Bones* this week, I'll never know. Alice Sebold is an amazing storyteller. I couldn't put the book down, but it's sad beyond words. It's not about Alzheimer's, but if you want some examples of how people deal with grief, take a look.

Abe's so thin. I've never seen him so thin. The hospice nurse just called to say she was there for lunch. He took a bite of jello, didn't drink anything. "He's looking more and more uncomfortable, physically uncomfortable," I tell her. "We can always give him more morphine," she offers. "Let's wait until I see him this afternoon," I say.

Tonight, 8:30 p.m.

Just home from Abe's, dog park, food shopping in that order. Emma especially, likes the long days.

Abe slept most of the time I was there, including through dinner, but he did wake up a few times to give me a partial smile. He also smiled at the aides when they came with the Vanderlift.

Yesterday, I went to Suzzallo for the first time in maybe a year. What a place. I went for an oral history workshop to get back in the spirit of interviewing for the book I'm supposed to be writing. I'm also taking a line break workshop. No, my dear children, not a dance class. Line breaking, as in poems.

March 28, 2009

Of pain & dying

The only other person I've seen as exhausted as Abe was last night was my mother. After six years of suffering from heart disease she died January 21, 1996 at the age of 96. In the days before she died she was as worn out and tired as anyone I'd ever seen. She weighed 70 pounds. She was in pain. She said she felt like "there is an elephant on my chest."

Abe looks uncomfortable, but he doesn't appear to be in pain. There is no elephant on his chest. His pain is of a different sort, just as mine is and yours is.

A hospice chaplain told my mother she could let go, she didn't have to hold on anymore. I thought that was an absurd statement to make to a dying person. Do we have control to *hang on* when we're dying any more than an insect does when it's dying? Mother said: "What do you mean don't hang on? I'm not doing anything to hang on. I just don't go anywhere."

Somewhere I read that family members' attention to dying people help them live longer, help them hold on. Who's the *them*, the dying? Or those watching the dying not die?

Every time I turn around people tell me to pray. I wish they'd stop.

Creatures live. Then they die. Everything else is story.

And wait.

March 29, 2009

Dental hygiene

We can't just wait, as I said yesterday, for the Alzheimer's patient to expire, though sometimes it feels as if that's what I'm doing. There are plenty of things still to learn about end-of-life care. Brushing the Alzheimer's patient's teeth is one of them.

Washington State law says nursing home personnel cannot force care on a patient, so when Abe refuses care—shakes his head, *no!*—the staff's hands are tied.

Abe loved to brush his teeth (he used Colgate) and took pride in it; he still has all but a couple of back teeth. My goal for today is not just to use the swab sticks but to brush his teeth like he used to (or almost). He'd want me to.

I'll bring two new tooth brushes, one for him and one for me, a fresh tube of his Colgate and a fresh tube of my Aquafresh. I'll find an extra one of those spit-in-things they keep in his room, and we'll brush our teeth together.

I don't know why I haven't thought of this before. Sometimes I get paralyzed, I think. He still holds so much power for me. And for others. He's not a doctor anymore (they call him Dr. Abe). He's a patient and needs his teeth brushed, darn it. Those swabs don't do the trick.

If the teeth brushing activity works, we'll go downstairs to see the canaries again—he loved them yesterday—and we'll both have sparkling teeth. Wish me luck!

March 31, 2009

Let me call you sweetheart

We did the tooth brushing; it worked, not a great job, but he followed my movements. He couldn't rinse and he only kept his mouth open for a couple go rounds and didn't spit till half an hour later, but we did it.

Afterwards went downstairs to watch the canaries. On the way, a visit to hear the chaplain sing and strum his guitar. He's always delightful, but when he got to "Let me call you Sweetheart," I lost it.

Went back upstairs to hear another staff member sing Hank Williams, all the while Abe drank orange juice and studied his placemat. He also ate a cookie.

I kissed him goodbye and stood watching in the doorway for awhile. Went across the street to the public library, checked out some books and came home at sixish. Crashed till now.

Taking Emma for a walk.

That's about all I can accomplish for today.

Tomorrow begins National Poetry Month.

April 1, 2009

Small annoyances, plus this & that

Don't say: You're good. I don't feel good. I feel like a *kvetch*, always complaining, if not aloud, inside myself, where I'm annoyed and angry with God.

It's not that we had such a great marriage. Sometimes, we fought like cats and dogs. Separated, got back together, made up, but all that seems irrelevant now. He's the most beautiful sight I see in a day. Not necessarily because I'm looking at someone I love (I love a lot of people) but because I'm witnessing a part of life that often goes unnoticed.

And there's more: I witness myself witnessing him. And I witness those who care for him and I'm grateful that we, as a society, don't put our old people out in the street to die, not as common practice anyway. And I witness people trying to do better, always.

Yesterday's mail included my contributor's copy of *Beyond Forgetting: Poetry and Prose about Alzheimer's Disease* edited by Holly J. Hughes, with a forward by Tess Gallagher. It's published by Kent University Press of Kent, Ohio. Thanks to Holly, Kent U and Tess for getting this out.

Twelve of us will be reading from *Beyond Forgetting* at the Frye Museum on May 3rd. 2 p.m. Try to make it. Bring your friends, I tell my friends.

April 6, 2009

Food, writing & your loved ones

I haven't wanted to write here.
I'm tired of the wait.
My interest is the poem,
especially the space
but space holds content.
So here I am again.

Visitors of patients—
this, you must know:
There was a birthday party.
For whom? The floor cat.
This cat is as big as a dog.
Emma doesn't understand it.
She keeps away.

There was a beautiful cake,
paw prints on white icing.
Who would have thought not to give a piece to Abe?
With it, he drank juice. I, coffee.
We smiled and listened to the music.
It was a good time.

The social worker called me into her office.
"If you're going to feed Abe when you're here,
you'll have to sign this release."
Turns out: when a patient is on a pureed diet,
he can't have anything but a pureed diet.
Otherwise, he might aspirate and the results could be fatal.

Of course I wouldn't sign the paper. How could I know I shouldn't give him a piece of cake when it's sitting right there in front of him, it's soft and delicious. I'm feeding him, it's going down, easily. He even had a soft cookie the day before. I gave it to him. He loved it and I loved him loving it. No one said he's not allowed. It's going down easily. Yes, easily. Can you imagine. He can swallow again. Or could on that day. At that time—3 p.m.—on that day.

Anyway, "omg, thanks for telling me. No, I'll never do that again." And gave her back the form.

Moral: If your loved ones in nursing homes are signed up to get one kind of diet, make sure you get permission before giving them anything else. Don't try oranges, a sandwich, candy, a pear. And for heaven's sake no matzos, even gefilte fish, for Passover next week. Or Easter bunnies either.

This is what I'm reading:

- *My Father's Brain* by Jonathan Franzen *in How to Be Alone* by Jonathan Franzen (New York: Farrar, Strauss and Giroux, 2002) pp. 7-38
- Thanks to faithful reader, Elisabeth Hanscomb, for the following reference: *Living Autobiographically: How We Create Identity in Narrative* by Paul John Eakin

April 10, 2009

Writing, technology & another good moment

I can't keep up with technology, even that which would help me manage my writing into respectably-looking computer files. I have a book manuscript here, another one there, and another in a file under the sink (so to speak). I look at Abe and think of all the technology he's not been privy to since he's been *gone,* out of the loop, in another place.

Back to 45 years ago, August 15, 1964, the day my father died: "He's never even heard *Fiddler on the Roof.* He hasn't heard 'If I Were a Rich Man'," which his bent shoulders sang every day. A thought "just out of the blue," as my mother would say.

I used to store such free-floating thoughts in notebooks that I carried around with me, and, now, 39 years of handwritten diaries, scribblings stacked in file cabinets and in closets upstairs. I intended to transfer them to the computer, but I see now that if I lived to be 120 I wouldn't finish transcribing one notebook, much less the lot of them.

Nor could I tackle my mother's diaries. I had planned to do that too, but finally I gave up and donated them to the archives in Special Collections at UW's Suzzallo library. Someone else will have to do that work.

All this as way of telling you: I found Joannie Stangeland. I know her as a poet (with a job) who's read for the It's About Time Writers Reading Series which I curate, but I didn't know she was a tech whiz. You've just got to watch her how-to-manage-your-writing videos. They actually made me relax.

-162-

No more asking the kids "perty pleeze bullet this for me." And maybe even no more emailing my daughter late at night whining: "could you please perty please change my references to APA style?"

But I will never ever stop asking my grandkids to update my cell phone addresses for me. I adore watching them use technology so easily, all the while they still even read books.

But the most important note of the day: When I walk into the dining room, Abe sees me right away. He smiles his best Alzheimer's smile, whispers: *Hi Sweetheart* and raises his lips to kiss me hello. Nothing gets better than that.

April 15, 2009

He was much better today. And thirsty. Drank two-and-a-half cups of pear juice.

I didn't *schlep* him up and down the elevator and through the halls to visit the canaries or the people in the other unit. Just sat with him and leafed through a garden book (which he took an interest in) and listened to a piano playing. I got up to leave after half an hour or so.

He puckered up as I kissed him goodbye, then immediately turned his head toward the people setting up for supper. When I left, he was smiling at the man sitting next to him.

April 15, 2009

Meltdown

I didn't go to see him yesterday. I worked on footnotes, made an actual dinner instead of eating out of a box, kept a doctor's appointment and laughed for three hours with a poet friend.

This, after the day before's "meltdown," as my daughter calls it—sat in my car in the nursing home parking lot and cried for half hour before going in. Abe would not want this for me.

So I took the day off and actually enjoyed cleaning up my footnotes. Maybe I'll even finish an essay tonight. I've only been working on it for a year. Wish me luck.

April 21, 2009

I haven't visited Abe since last Thursday. I got sick and couldn't go in with sore throat and fever. I still have a cold so won't go for another few days. There's a sign on the front door of the nursing home telling visitors: "Leave your colds at home." So here I am in a week that doesn't include Alzheimer visits.

Only trouble is I've forgotten what that kind of week looks like. I have to feed the dog and take her out—she doesn't care if I'm sneezing. And I have to do my work, which in my line—writing—can be accomplished by night or day, dripping nose or not. But what do I do during the time I usually see Abe?

Besides checking in with the nursing staff, I go through his clothes. It's time to give them away. Normally this wouldn't take place until after death, but this death has been going on a long time, and someone can make good use of them. Plus, they're taking up room in the closet.

Neither of these reasons is the real truth, of course. The truth is: I can't bear looking at them anymore. They're so big they'd swallow up the little man he's become, physically little, that is.

Lisa, Abe's youngest daughter, came up from California last week with grandson Ray. During her visit she helped me take her dad's clothes out of the closet. She folded his pants and jackets and put them on the chair beside the black garbage bags I planned to put them in. Community Services for the Blind called: Write "Blind" on the front of the bag. And then it's done.

But it's not done. I don't put the clothes in the bags. When Lisa and Ray leave, I unfold the suits and go through the pockets. In a jacket that hadn't been cleaned and that he wore most recently, I find dog treats and a neatly-folded paper napkin. I give Emma the treats and throw the napkin away—there's no smell in it.

This is getting too hard. It was easier when Lisa was here—even with her tears. Or maybe because of them.

Ok, enough!

I give up the notion of writing a poem recounting each article's history, place Abe's things in the black garbage bags and put them outside on the bench for CSB to collect. That was 7 a.m. yesterday. By 10 a.m. they were gone. So was the rest of the day.

But I'm here now and moving on, however slowly. As Lisa says: "What else can we do?"

It's nice to be part of a *we*, isn't it.

April 26, 2009

Thirty Seconds Before Dinner

He was different tonight
more withdrawn
though he did raise his arm
when he saw a motorcycle
hanging on the wall.
You wouldn't expect
to see a Harley-Davidson
in a nursing home
but this Harley flew
out of the picture frame
as if it were a bird.
Abe was astonished,
even though his facial muscles
remained tight
and his mouth stayed closed.
For thirty seconds his eyes lit up.
Afterwards, we returned to where we were before:
me wondering what to do next,
he not waiting to go to dinner.

May 2, 2009

Spouse as Home

I didn't know he
was my *shul*
my language
my mother tongue
and prayer
the *zeyde* I lost,
and *bubbes*
I never had.
Or that he was my homeland.
And exile.
My nakedness.

I didn't know
when I met him
thirty years ago
that I had needed
a place to
dwell
in.
Or that knowing
turned less
into more
And more
into
less.

Oh,
where
shall I dwell
when he's
gone

Where
shall
I
when
he's

May 3, 2009

Frye Art Museum
At the very moment I honor him, do I not betray him?

> *It's a dangerous mission. You*
> *could die out there. You*
> *could go on forever.*
> Tess Gallagher, "Instructions to the Double"

As soon as I go to the podium, I want Abe. In my mind, I run to the nursing home to be with him. I don't belong in this space. Something is wrong. I'm supposed to talk about my poem "Spouse as Home" but I can't speak. I can't look at my notes. What I'm doing is unethical. My body tells me this.

I want to shout: **Abe is still alive.** He's only a half-hour away. How can I stand up here talking about our relationship in story when he's flat on his back in a nursing home? If not flat on his back, then in a wheelchair; if not in a wheelchair, then in a Vanderlift being transferred from bed to chair or from chair to bed. All the while, I cash in, so to speak, on his misfortune.

I want to tell the audience that "my presence here before you betrays my husband." But I don't say this and I remain where I am, as if making art out of pain is a perfectly ok thing to do. And, of course, it is. I know this. It's essential, and Abe would agree.

Beyond Forgetting: Poetry and Prose About Alzheimer's is essential. As contributor, Denise Calvetti Michaels, a Cascade Community College psychology teacher, said to me after the reading: "We must use this book in the Humanities. It's the text to use." *Beyond Forgeting* is in the world, thanks to editor Holly J. Hughes, and I'm proud that a poem of mine has been included; yet, here at the Frye where we're celebrating the book's launch, standing at this podium, I feel that in some sense I'm betraying Abe, who for better or worse was always my friend. I know I'm not betraying him; on the other hand, I'm not convinced.

Moreover, if I were to say what's on my mind, wouldn't I betray the artists next to me and the audience who came to see us? And if I were to cut my art off from my own life would I not be betraying myself? What is art if not an expression of life, and of self and other?

Sophomoric questions. They have been discussed before. There's a whole literature on the downside of creating art out of someone else's pain or even out of one's own pain. Theodore Adorno wrote that "writing poetry after Auschwitz is barbaric." Perhaps it is, but it's also essential.

Poetry is a means, not just an end. It's a way to understand the awfulness of life and to use that awfulness as a tool for growth and change. Tess Gallagher said in her introduction to our reading, "We can fail, get up and try again." If I interpret her comments correctly, poetry then, is a place where one can fail. And this is good.

Finally, when I did speak—and I did manage a few words between all my *uhmms*—I felt that Abe and I were together on the podium, aphasia notwithstanding.

Abe is still here. He breathes. He lives. He doesn't eat much because he's forgotten how to swallow; but he eats some, and he drinks a lot. He's here and alive and smiles (when he can) and experiences joy and, therefore, is. He experiences pain and, therefore, is. He still knows.

When I walked in his room the other day, he lit up and said *I love. . . you Swee. . . ar.* He lives in the world with us. This is what I wanted to say through my *uhmms.* I'm afraid of objectifying him.

I'll say it next time, and there will be a next time because writing this today, working through and coming to the end here instructs me to share what I know about Alzheimer's disease for the benefit of those Abes for whom Dr. Arthur Ginzberg, a Seattle neurologist and another of *Forgetting's* contributors, says do have hope.

With further research there is hope, and as ambivalent as I am, as scared as I am—and I'm scared a lot of the time—I'll continue to share what I know in the best way I know, and that's by being part of a writing community that works not to betray, but to teach and to learn, as *Beyond Forgetting* does. As I do. I can say that now.

May 13, 2009

I haven't seen him in more than a week. I walk in his room. It's 1:30 pm. He's sleeping, I stay a few minutes, kiss him on the forehead and leave. The next day I arrive at 3:30, a better time. He's in the community/dining room. One other patient's there. She's on the other side of the room, in a wheelchair, head down. Abe sees me for the first time in ten days. He's been told I've had a cold, but nothing seems to matter. There's no distance between us.

He's beautiful. His eyes are clear. His beard is full again. He smiles as if there is nothing wrong with him, except he happens to be sitting in a wheelchair, and, well, a few other things. He's pulled one pant leg up and is examining the pant material. He's engrossed in the hemline, captivated, but he's also aware that I've pulled up a chair to sit next to him.

I can't believe how well he looks. The chart says he's gained six pounds. I can tell. His skin is shiny, and baby-skin pink. This man is thriving. Why do they keep telling me he's in the last six months of his life? I don't get it. Abe is not dying any more than anyone else is and just as everyone else is. He's happy, not just resigned; he's content, even flourishing. He experiences sadness. He sees the woman sitting across the room, head down and alone, except she's not alone. She's with him, now us. He experiences joy.

Alzheimer's is a fantastical place to inhabit, as visitor or resident. It's powerful, contains meanings I don't pretend to understand. Maybe I shouldn't try. But I'm confused. I'm so confused my head is spinning. Hospice has been wonderful for Abe and for me, but the premise that he'll die within six months keeps me in limbo, waiting, disconcerted, baffled, afraid. I put off visiting the children, giving an out-of-town poetry reading, teaching a class, taking a ferry. Any minute I think something might happen. I can't keep living my life this way.

Abe is wonderful. I'm so proud of him I want to climb up on a rooftop and shout: **Look at this man!** He is not violent or mean. He doesn't throw things or yell. He is not an Alzheimer's stereotype. There is no Alzheimer's stereotype. He interacts with people. He's civil. When I wheel him into the music room where all the people are, he's visibly touched. I know this. I know this even more when the folk singer at the front of the room begins singing "We Shall Overcome" and Abe looks at me with a kind of glee I haven't seen for such a long while. He reaches for my hand and his face sings with me.

May 16, 2009

New York Son's Here

When I told Abe
Scott's coming
he'll have a new visitor today,
Abe said:
And an important one at that.

He still
feels
the
connection.

What a blessing.

May 17, 2009

The most incredible of days

There are some days that I'm so blown away by Abe's doings that I come home knowing I'm done for the day. Maybe even the next day. Not only do I not have the energy for anything else, there's nothing else I can accomplish or be a part of that equals what I've experienced in Abe's presence, truly a different aspect of humanity.

Sometimes he blossoms.
Even in the absence of sun,
he blossoms.

Yehuda Amichai writes:
"To forget and blossom, to blossom and forget
is all."

Can we ask for more
but to blossom?

What's happening in Abe's mind—what he communicates and doesn't communicate—takes my breath away. Here's an example:

One day last week when we actually had sun here in Seattle, I took Abe outside on the patio. He, in his wheelchair. I, on the bench in front of him. I had the pocketbook—practically a suitcase—with me that he bought me about twenty years ago, one of those times he went to a medical conference and I was in school and couldn't go with him, or didn't want to go with him.

He became preoccupied with the pocketbook. Inside, stuff: purse, glasses, cell phone, books, pens, a journal. I was holding a pen. He took the pen. In the meantime, he's saying words. I write them down:

It's such a nice . . .
You didn't finish, I say.
No, I didn't, he says right back
I'll just . . .
I have to . . .

I turn the journal to an empty page and hand it to him.

First he draws a line that begins to look like a face and speaks more words, including:

You're cute.

I won't forget that.

Or: *Thank you for this beautiful . . .* [day]

The most exciting and fascinating piece of script is the straighter line at the top of the page. He drew that second and after he drew it, or wrote it, he looked at me and said: *This is what I'm thinking.* I sat astonished. *This is what I'm thinking.* For the next few days everyone I saw had to hear this story.

This is what I'm thinking.

Millie folds her hands over her heart. Wendy and Pat ask: What does it mean? It means he's thinking. He's aware. He's making connections.

There's so much inside him that we don't know, that doctors and scientists don't know. How important for researchers to work with individuals, use examples from their lives, next to all the graphs and statistics mounted on a page.

Readers write to tell me they admire my devotion to Abe. I don't know if what I feel is devotion. Would you say you were devoted to your left leg or right arm? What I feel is a wonderful (though difficult) kind of attachment. There's no release from my interaction with this human being's beingness, his essence.

What happens with Abe takes over my body, and I have to wait until the blood flow gets going again before I can take one more step out of myself and into the world. Good thing I'm not like this with my children, though I probably was when they were babies. I like to watch minds develop and, as it turns out, I like to watch them go through permutations, transformation and change. This is the way it is for me. I didn't ask for it. Abe certainly didn't. It's just the way it is.

Note:
Amichai's quote comes from his poem "Sadness of the Eyes and Descriptions of a Journey" in his book *Amen*, as quoted by Emily Warn in *Shadow Architect*, p. 51.

This is what I'm reading

- *Phantoms in the Brain: Probing the Mysteries of the Human Mind.* by V. S. Ramachandran and Sandra Blakeslee
- *The Book of Laughter and Forgetting* by Milan Kundera
- *Poetry as Travel Journal* by Yehuda Amichai

May 26, 2009

Patience

I know I haven't written here in a while, but I haven't had much to say. What does one say when a condition lasts forever? Every day the same report, the same story. One day he's up, one day he's down. One day his weight is 160, a week later it's 163; the next, it's 157, then up again to 160. One day a tooth falls out. The next day, another. One day you walk in and he's smiling in his wheelchair, the next day he's sleeping in his wheelchair. One day he's in the community room picking at his clothes, the next day he's lying in his pee.

He's lying in his pee and I don't know what to do. I can't pick him up and hold him in my arms. I can't change him. I can't even lie down next to him. All I can do, the only thing we can do, is wait for the nurse's aide and Abe's not on the schedule right now. So I get some lotion and moisten his face, his hands and legs. Our grandchild joins me. We massage his feet, his toes. We three talk awhile, such as we can. He with his aphasia, me and the child in our uncertainty. He smiles and, finally, our grandchild and I kiss him goodbye.

Is this something to write about? I'm not sure anymore. Except to note Abe's patience. He has so much patience.

May 28, 2009

He called me Esther

Abe is no longer gravely ill. There is no reason to stand by and watch his teeth fall out. I don't care if he is on hospice. I took him to the dentist. No surprise: Decay. I made a second appointment.

Today when I took him into the TV room, he was his old snarly self. In so many words and non-words, he said: *Get me out of here.* I wheeled him into a non-Oprah-hour room, gave him a book to hold, and he relaxed. That's when he called me *Esther.*

May 30, 2009

When I walked into his room he was sitting in the wheelchair staring. His eyes were red, and I thought he had been crying, but there were no tears. He didn't know me. I looked straight into him and said: "Hi Abe. I'm Esther. I'm your wife. I'm Esther."

Really?

"Really," I said.

And he was alive again.

I wheeled him down the hall where I knew I could find him a strawberry shake. Found coffee for me, juice and a shake for him. Wheeled us into an out-of-the-way room where no one was talking and a TV wasn't on and fed us. I had him back.

Then I took us downstairs to see the canaries. Afterwards we visited the Alzheimer's unit where he lived last year, found the outdoor patio empty and went outside. The sun was beautiful. 80 degrees in Seattle.

We studied the herb garden, picked a buttercup, hugged some friends and went back upstairs. By then it was nearly dinner time. I kissed him goodbye. He smiled and said: . . . *love* . . .

June 1, 2009

. . . and so he sleeps

I arrived at Abe's today at 1:30, a couple hours earlier than usual. I knew he'd be sleeping but the kids went early yesterday and woke him up, quite successfully. I thought I'd try too. Besides I'd spent the last two hours in a bookstore piddling around and having lunch with a friend, so I wanted to get home early to get some writing done.

When he's sleeping he looks like a baby, like the kids when they were so quietly asleep in their beds after a long day. They could do nothing wrong. Neither can he.

I'm afraid I'm making a saint out of him. I've forgotten every problem or conflict we ever had. No doubt I'm rewriting our history. I can't help it. How we are now is part of our story too, isn't it? Or is it just my story?

I nudge him a tad, tell him who I am, kiss him, say: "Hi." He says *Hi* back and smiles. I'm always so delighted when he smiles. I didn't think he'd ever get his smile back and I'd have to look at pictures to see it again.

Remember all those months ago when he forgot how to smile? Around the same time he forgot, or so it seemed, how to swallow? Now he not only smiles, he even swallows more.

The brain, the brain. Oh, that wonderful and forbidding brain. Three pounds of mystery.

I kiss him again and say: "I'll see you later. I'll let you sleep."

Good, he says.

He returns to sleep and to whatever world he lives in. I leave the room, thank the staff and return to the world I live in.

June 14, 2009

Abe's 81st birthday

I walked in yesterday to balloons tied around his wheelchair and the bluegrass folk singer singing "Happy Birthday Dr. Abe."

His lips reached to kiss me. He touched my shoulder, my neck. When the music ended I wheeled him to another room, one with more breeze. He ate a cup of orange sherbet, drank a glass of heath shake and talked to me in a language neither of us knows.

I found a copy of the *Smithsonian*, showed him Eudora Welty's photographs from the 1930s, told him she was a photographer long before she won the Pulitzer. He seemed to like that.

Maybe he remembered the photos he used to take. They're in shoe boxes and desk drawers. After he retired I urged him to pursue photography as a second career. He knew a lot about light, shadow, but, he said: *This is for fun.*

Today I want to bring him a birthday present, but I don't know what to bring. He was always a man who needed little of the material. Alois Alzheimer (1864-1915), another pathologist, was born on June 14th. I imagine these two medical doctors—Abe and Alois—in a lab together, working on a brain.

This is what I'm reading:

- just finished *Kite Runner* by Khaled Hosseini
  —couldn't put it down
- Now his *A Thousand Splendid Suns*—can put it down

September, 2009

A Week

Monday
I just came back from Abe's.
He's still the same: wheelchair bound,
speaks few words.
I didn't stay long.
He was at a men's club meeting,
sleeping.

Tuesday
It's warm outside but not warm enough to take him out.
I wheel him to the window
to see the sun.
He smiles
when a bus goes by,
laughs at a woman
with books in her arms,
points.

Wednesday
Last night he said a whole sentence,
Look who's here!
Another day while lying in bed,
he said: *I'm scared.*
That same evening, he asked:
Are you healthy?

Thursday

In the parking lot, I look
up toward the television room
where I left him watching.
He sees me. I wave
and he waves
back.
I can't believe
he's responding. I jump up
and down and we wave
and wave.
Here we are
a married couple still—
me in the parking lot
he upstairs in the nursing home—
waving
(to each other)
as if there's no tomorrow.
I want to run back up to him,
but I continue waving,
and waving.
I don't know how to move.
I don't know how
to get in my car.

Friday

Maybe tomorrow, I'll take him outside.

Saturday
I don't think I'll go today

Sunday
I didn't see him
yesterday
or the day before.
(Oh, yes I did, I saw him
Thursday).
Today,
when he saw me
he said,
You're good
and fell back to sleep.
Then I left.

September 10, 2009

And

when I leave him
and know I won't be back
for days at a time—
my heart asks
why
why

December 12, 2009

A grandchild is
a blessing on the planet
a halo, and more—

December 29, 2009

Him and Me

We're at the game table
I give him a domino
He puts it in his mouth

I start to write *my mouth*
He puts it in my mouth.

Sometimes
I can't
distinguish
the difference
between
him
and
me

How much of him
is
me
and how much of me
is
him

I don't understand:
We didn't even get along
that well

2010

January 10, 2010

No Pits

Here's a poem I found on my computer from June 27, 2003. I remember the exact moment I wrote it. We were in the kitchen. He was sitting at the table reading the newspaper. I was writing. There was a bowl of Satsuma oranges between us. I looked up at him. He looked so content, I couldn't believe anything was wrong with him. I thought I was making things up.

Small things make him happy:
A newspaper article. The next door neighbor's
funny hat. A bus ride downtown. A bowl
of Satsuma oranges without pits. Mad Magazine.
A park bench. The children. Me.

March 23, 2010

Yesterday afternoon

He was at the men's club meeting, so I stayed only a few minutes. A minister runs the group. They were talking about health care. No surprise. Congratulations, Mr. President!

Abe's the only one in the group with Alzheimer's. I have no idea what he understands, but he seemed to be listening.

April 7, 2010

I find no small talk
here in all this garbling
bees pollinating flowers

Alzheimer's disease—
Nature's unforgiving kiss
neurons unblossomed

watching them I see
the brain is like a flower
petals fall too soon

April 13, 2010

In the TV room, after lunch, before his afternoon nap

Out the window
we see a dog
with a red jacket on
Inside
Abe laughs
and takes my hand

Out the window
parked cars
and a cabulance
I squeeze Abe's hand

It's been a good visit
until the aide comes in
and it's time for me
to extract
my hand.

January 15, 2010

His face, almost

His face was small tonight
I could hold it in one hand.
His skin was pale, white almost.
His arms were slack
I took his hands.

I helped him move his arms
and we danced with them,
up and down
we danced with them, his arms
he in his wheelchair
me on a stool beside.

He laughed, almost. He laughed
and I could have cried
but I waited until I was
outside and then
his face became large,
large, I tell you,
like a full moon.

How did that happen?

His face was small
I could hold it in my hand, almost
but, now, driving away
his face is large. Really.
It floats in front of me
like a moon.

April 18, 2010

Color

—for Abe

Today you are
the color
of pink
unlike yesterday
when your
color
was blue
and I thought
death
was
imminent.
Doctors
don't
know.
No one does.
You could
live
a long
other life
sitting
in your
wheelchair
smiling.

April 23, 2010

Penny Harvest Youth Philanthropy Summit

I attended the Penny Harvest Youth Philanthropy Summit yesterday at the Seattle Center. Caregiving may keep me from many events, but no way was I going to miss this. My granddaughter's on the youth board and I went as a chaperone.

Penny Harvest is one of thirty programs sponsored by Solid Ground, a community service organization (some may remember them as the Fremont Public Association). Now based in Seattle's Wallingford neighborhood, Solid Ground helps "over 38,000 households each year to overcome poverty and build better futures throughout King County and beyond."

Penny Harvest is awesome, I can tell you. I served lunch. I saw. I sat in on student-run caucuses, one led by my eleven-year old granddaughter. I watched as groups of children developed arguments to promote their choices of causes to give money to: homelessness, hunger, Haiti, the environment, animal and child abuse. I was at the summit from 9 a.m. until 2 p.m and not once was there a disturbance, much less a fight among the kids. Our legislators should do as well.

Children from all different walks of life, from private and public schools, from elementary school through high school, from every religion and color of the rainbow together learning skills to become leaders in their communities. A parent couldn't ask for more, not from neighborhood activists nor from teachers who guide these kids to learn in the context of public and global need.

I'm worried that due to the economic downturn, the program will have to shut its doors and the youth board that was created yesterday won't be able to serve next year. I spend a lot of my time with the elderly, and the sick elderly, as you well know. These folks are some of our weakest links, those who need the most from the rest of us. The kids I observed at Penny Harvest Youth Philanthropy Summit are already in the business of helping our weakest links. Let us adults help them.

April 27, 2010

Abe didn't call me back

In my dream last night
Abe didn't call me back.
A whole weekend went by
with no word.
When I awaken he's
in a nursing home,
dead; yet,
not dead.
Sick people
surround him.
Some scream
for their children.
Some for parents
or a lost cat.
One woman looks
for her sister.
A man in a wheel
chair sings a song.
Abe smiles at
everyone.

May 5, 2010

On Poetry, Peace, & How Long Has He Had Alzheimer's?

Every time I'm asked, as I was today: "How long has Abe had Alzheimer's?" I say about a decade, but I can't pinpoint it. Around 2001 maybe, after his hip surgery, when he was vulnerable and couldn't fight back, but I don't know. I used to think I was making it up, and why wouldn't I when he could put together words like these below.

The date of Abe's poem here reminds me that even though Alzheimer's was invading our home by 2002, the disease had not yet destroyed Abe's language center. I had asked him if he would write something for a worldwide poetry day program that I was emceeing at the Seattle Public library, and he gave me this poem. I wish I could remember his reading it aloud. I can't, but at least I have a record of this phase of his history within the context of Alzheimer's disease.

A poem can bring peace: a pleasant thought indeed

by Abe Schweid

In childhood,
I accepted language's power.
I knew words could hurt.
So why not let them heal?

Now, full-grown, I've lost touch
with that faith.
Others carry on, their dictionaries
filled with meaning.

Trapped in a downward spiral
the world is again at war.
Body piled on body with
no end in sight.

Whose bizarre encryption
defies my childhood dream
that a poem can bring peace!

Written for "Dialogue Among Civilizations Through Poetry," March
2002, in which poets addressed the question: Can poetry help bring
about a culture of peace & non-violence in the world?

May 6, 2010

At the nursing home, after lunch

Blossoms on the window pane
Tree limbs scratching glass—

A ladybug crawls
around a leaf's edge—it falls
on a flower's wing

Quiet makes us laugh
clouds keep us company
sky is blue today

but crows keep us vigilant

May 7, 2010

Husband

I wish you'd change
your ways
just for today
so we could
speak to
each other's
ear

Your lack
is like a leaf
falling
Even so
I'm glad we met
two East Coast Jews
in Seattle
where else
might we
be
might we

I'm glad you're here
I can touch your face
your skin
I like to comb
your hair

your eyes
hold me still

The last two weeks

I haven't heard him speak
a word
in the last two weeks
but today
when we were sitting
together
in the quiet
of an out-of-the-way
room
after I finished
cutting his mustache
and beard
he said:
I'm sorry, honey,
as if he knew exactly
what we'd gone through
all these years.

June 13, 2010

Abe's not doing well.

He has pneumonia and congestive heart failure. The days and hours are iffy. I think it's best to call off class for the time being. The hospice nurse said she didn't think Abe would hold out until the kids came in two weeks so they're starting to come sooner. Lisa's flying in Tuesday. Ian and family starting up from California also Tuesday.

Same day

The Word "Other"

As you lie in bed I
look for you
in the word other
I remember how you used to be
with me inside you, the other -
accessible and to the touch
you were
any time of day
or night
your skin
so silken
and male.
Now you are
an in-
accessible other
holding difference
of another kind.

Your sense of self
hood
nearly dead
mine lost in what we used to be
each of us afloat
separate
without a will
and un-
remembering
how to see
without the other
and without a hint
of how to see together
what we've become
without
the other.

June 14, 2010

Abe's birthday

I've signed papers for hospice care. He has pneumonia and conges-tive heart failure. As of a few minutes ago, his heart rate was as high as 160. Temperature, even with Tylenol, is over 101.

Right now he's comfortable. The Foss staff treat him as family. Hospice means more hands on board—nurses, social worker, chap-lain—a caring team he's had before. The kids are coming in. I'll keep you posted. I can't wait to see them.

Today is Abe's birthday. He's 82.

June 2010-
December 2012
Part 4

After His Death

June 15, 2010

That Day

Your eyes determined to reach the destination
you have started towards.

Your face, surprisingly aglow, teaching me
the meaning of ascendance.

One adult child beside the bed,
the others on their way.

In your ear, I say the *Sh'ma*.
I say I love you.

Your tongue works slowly
side to side.

Outside, a mild annoyance:
a tree branch scratching the window pane.

I must remember this day of your dying—the wait,
as you fight up hill, to go

to wherever it is people go
when they die a valiant death

such as yours,
my love.

June 15, 2010

We buried him.

June 16, 2010

shiva

June 24, 2010

I can get mad at him again

I don't have to go to the nursing home anymore. I don't even have
to think about going. Not today, not tomorrow. Not next week. And
I can get mad at him again. Isn't that an odd thing to be thinking?
I didn't get mad at him the whole time he was in the nursing home,
three years and ten months. Not once, a contrast—you can be sure—
from before he became ill.

I can't understand how life can go on as usual. Busses run, shoppers
shop, the grocery store on the corner still stands. Starbucks hasn't
gone out of business. Facebook flourishes. Yet Abe is in the ground.
He's wrapped in a shroud. He has his *tallis* on. He's gone. He
flickered on earth for a while, and then he left.

While I'm still at his bedside asking him for one more breath, I have
him back with me as he used to be; and he's saying to all who knew
and loved him: *Thank you. You helped me through.* To me he's saying, as
he did when I was watching the shovels of dirt hit his coffin: *You did
it, Babe. You got me buried, and I'm proud.*

Now I have to remember how I used to be before he got sick. The
sound of my voice is unfamiliar. The name of the day. Time is
different. I didn't realize there were so many hours to use as I wish.
My life is trying to reach me, before I sleep. I think it will.

October 8, 2010

Seattle Art Museum

Dear Abe,

Sometimes I write letters to you. It's a way for me to get to know
us better, to remember us in the past, the way we were and the way I
thought we were.

Tonight I'm at the Picasso exhibit watching a biography of us
sprawled across the walls,
an elbow here, an arm there. This one's tit, that one's splat. I sit in
front of "Self-Portrait in Straw Hat"
and watch Picasso
's eyes. You
on one side
him
on the other
and the beard I ran my fingers through,
not Picasso's stubble, hard. Metallic.
Mean. Who can forget the suicides:
        Olga's and Jacqueline's.
The Doras.

We spoke of that: You and I.
Today I found an old journal entry.

It says:
"He recognizes me.
He knows
he's
in a nursing home."

Abe, I'm afraid
I won't remember
your touch
will be
beyond my reach.
You'll fade away
like my parents did
like my sister did
slowly
before I
knew—
the blue period
the rose
the old guitarist
and the dance of veils.

Oh Abe

Death

is like a canvas
nailed
to the wall
an ice cream
cone in Picasso's hand
missing teeth

a green tongue
a kiss
your own straw hat

    and the pedestal
    table
    on which
    I write.

My darling
    goodnight.

November 19, 2010

Finding a new routine

It's five months since Abe died and little by little I'm finding a new routine. It's not easy, and my steps are small. I think of the nursing home vigil pretty much every day, and at times it seems my body longs to go back to that scenario, to mingle with patients and staff in the dining room and wander the halls waiting for this social worker or that. I went back a couple of times and will go again this holiday season, but for the most part, I'm scared of the place. Scared I'll end up there myself. I wonder how many caregivers of Alzheimer's patients come away from the caregiving experience feeling the same.

I find I'm resistant to listening to anything having to do with Alzheimer's, even good stuff like the wonderful program at the Frye "Museum, Making Art Accessible to People with Alzheimer's." I knew it would be wonderful but I couldn't bring myself to go. Turns out it's a good thing. A friend of mine went and when she read me some of the poems used in the workshops, I felt my body screaming. Is there no other world out there?

I finished up my work for the Jack Straw program, continue curating the It's About Time Reading Series—signing people up to read and emceeing. Sent out a few poems, got a few rejections—even a really nice one—teach my class and work on my book, but it's not enough and I'm not ready for my mind and body to take steps to do more. I guess that will come.

I have to pick out Abe's gravestone and I don't want to. I haven't gone back to the cemetery since we buried him. My mother's buried a few rows up, and I don't want to see her that way either.

I don't want to say prayers over their graves or bring them flowers or place stones on their headstones, as is the Jewish custom. I feel like a spoiled brat who didn't get her way. I want to throw a tantrum and say life's not fair, but we all know that.

Meanwhile, Alzheimer's research continues at a glowing pace. Support groups are on the scene as never before, and I guess we're all doing the best we can with the resources available to us. I didn't want to do Thanksgiving this year, but I'm ending up with a big turkey to cook and a house full of guests, Life is good. We just have to get used to it.

November 26, 2010

"Dear Doctor" Letters

First thing this morning after Thanksgiving, the ACLU calls for
Abe to give another donation. If it's not the ACLU, it's NARAL or
Planned Parenthood, or the Democratic Party or the Simon Wiesen-
thal Center or Cornell Alumni, or Doctors Without Borders or a
Native American Indian Center or an ambulance service in Israel. He
wrote checks to everybody.

In addition to those and the "normal" everyday junk mail requests,
I get Dear Doctor letters advertising microscopes, office furniture,
laboratory supplies, surgical instruments and, of course, magazines.
How many times do I have to contact this society or that to remind
them that Dr. Schweid died in June?

I know it's nobody's fault, other than the marketing companies, but
it's hard to keep telling people that your loved one doesn't live here
anymore.

December 2, 2010

Poem for my 69th birthday

Age

I look in the mirror
at my naked body
and see my mother Anna
and my aunts Mamie and Vivian,
even my cousin Anita.
And I smile at the beauty of age
and the women
I didn't know
until now they have died
and I am
they.

I'm not sure if Alzheimer's caregiving has made me feel old(er) or I
would have felt the same regardless. I do think it's taken its toll. Yet, I
see Abe's face in my hands at the moment of his death and I'm grate-
ful for that piece of time between us and for the years leading up to
it.

2011

August 8, 2011

I Sat Upon His Grave

I watched the letters of his name
upon the stone.

I cried until they came alive—
the letters of his name.

The grass was warm beneath me.

My face was hot
from the sun.

I rose to say goodbye
and touch his name.

The cemetery
transmogrified.

the ground swelled

His arms reached out to me—
and I was home.

September 2, 2011

I'm off to California
for the weekend,
leaving Emma
and pictures
of Abe
to a house
sitter

September 6, 2011

Meeting a blog-reader in a California bookstore

I don't study site stats. I write because I need to and try not to let numbers interfere with my work. Whatever I'm doing, whether earning a BA, MA, or Ph.D. while raising my children, whether I'm working at Sears or a social service agency, or teaching, or being Grandma, I write because my mind goes to the page. It lands there —in someone else's words or in my own.

I don't know who reads my writing. So I was pleasantly surprised this weekend when I met a woman who actually reads my blog. Both her parents have Alzheimer's. She found my site a couple years ago while looking for online resources. We became Facebook friends and discovered that she lives in the same town as my son, Ian, and, eerier still, she and Ian had worked together in a teachers' summer writing institute.

Yesterday Ian, the kids, and I went to the bookstore to check out Rick Riordan's adventure stories. I'd not heard of this author or of many of the authors the kids mention. I like when my grandchildren educate me, which is all the time, but for now I leave the younger generations to their own devices and wander over to the Women's Studies section ("old school," I'm told). I overhear a woman asking for a title I can't quite make out, but it sounds interesting and so does she. (Later I learn the book's title: *I Am an Emotional Creature: The Secret Life of Girls Around the World* by Eve Ensler).

I go back to the kids. My son sees a friend he took a class with. Esther! she calls out. His friend is not only the woman from the Women's Studies section, she's also the woman who reads my blog.

We hug and cry, and we talk Alzheimer's. After we part, I go to the restroom and cry more, not because I met a stranger whose life was impacted by my writing and who also knows my son, but because I see that I've been depriving myself of Alzheimer's Speak. In June (a year after Abe's death), I stopped seeing the grief counselor, and I haven't re-enlisted in the grief group I was in. I had enough of Alzheimer's and wanted to "move on." I was wrong (and not wrong).

I dislike the term "move on." It has nothing to do with healing or the reality of grief. Alzheimer's is a place, and one can't give up place. I can no more remove myself from Alzheimer's than I can renounce my hometown, Baltimore—however difficult it is to view the boarded up houses on streets where I skated and played kick ball. Place is an emotional space, which is as big as a city.

On the way home to Seattle last night, I read some of Barbara King-solver's *Small Wonder*. In her Forward she writes: "It is possible to move away from a vast, unbearable pain by delving into it deeper and deeper—by 'diving into the wreck,' to borrow . . . words from Adrienne Rich."

I use my writing to dive into the wreck. I also have a tendency to push the wreck away, to stomp on it, by writing about a subject out-side myself, such as a biographical subject. The experience of meet-ing my blog friend—the emotion I felt while speaking Alzheimer's with her—tells me that I can't pull away, that I need to develop more skill in balancing pleasure and pain—honor the pleasure of making new friends, for instance—with the pain of remembering. In the process I will learn more about my thirty-year relationship with Abe and how its bits and pieces came to be.

Kingsolver writes: "You can look at all parts of a terrible thing until you see that they're assemblies of smaller parts, all of which you can name, and some of which you can heal or alter, and finally the terror that seemed unbearable becomes manageable. I suppose what I'm describing is the process of grief."

I think so. Kingsolver's not off the hook yet, and neither am I. None of us is, and maybe we shouldn't be. There are different ways to examine conflict, new narratives to develop. We must discover them. At least, I must.

September 23, 2011

Found Nursing Home Poem 2007

I'm trying to discard things in my life that I don't need—old clothes
that have been hanging in the closet for twenty years, for instance.
They seem to be waiting for me to melt down to the size I used to
be—won't happen. Then there are the shoes I never wear but think
I might—I won't. And furniture I don't sit in. And a broken mirror
that makes me look thin—I'm not. And so on. I won't part with the
books I haven't looked at in thirty years, but I am rearranging them
so they're not scattered under the wrong subject headings. As for the
scraps of paper I haven't yet tucked into my loose leaf notebooks,
here's a poem I found in a stack of junk mail. I'll save it.

I lean down to kiss him hello
and wonder if he knows me enough
to be comfortable
with the physical closeness
I have thrust upon him.

Is holding his hand
or rubbing his arm
or massaging his neck
(he seems so weary)
acts too
familiar?

Am I taking liberties
with him?

An aide walks by
and he knows her
better
than he knows me.
Still, when I get up to leave
I kiss him
goodbye
not as I used to
but I kiss
him.

October 2, 2011

"Pantouming"

I've created a neologism—Pantouming. A pantoum is a poetic exercise whose repetition and freedom, along with structure, is particularly helpful in achieving distance from, and closeness, to grief. Last week I wrote about twenty-five pantoums. Publishable or not, the process of writing in form helped me understand what I needed to know. Here's one with some explanation. I grew up in a Jewish family of leftists, with the ubiquitous Orthodox segment. Part of me always wished I could be like the religious girls who never seemed to question existence or have conflicts about beingness. Abe was raised in an Orthodox family. He started *cheder* (Hebrew school) at three years old and knew "everything." He had a gorgeous cantorial voice. I went to *shul* just to hear him sing. And now:

I hear him *daven* in my sleep

His memory clings to me
I hear him *daven* in my sleep
Even those Alzheimer's years
are mine to keep.

I hear him *daven* in my sleep
His voice fills the *shul*
Those years are mine to keep
His davening a jewel.

His voice fills the *shul*
He was never off key
His davening was a jewel.
His memory clings to me

He was never off key
He knew his people and who he was.
in spite of the Alzheimer years,
his memory clings to me.

daven=to pray
shul=synagogue

October 3, 2011

Writing in form helps with grief

The pantoum was so helpful to me that next I tried the sonnet form. I probably won't visit it again for a while but, like "pantouming," the repetition of sonnet-writing helped me understand why I couldn't stop crying. It forced me to look at the grief I was experiencing and to articulate it, if not to others, then to Abe on the page.

Sonnet for Abe

My love for you continues to this day.
With our photographs and history I stay.
Writing stories of our life together
keeps me brave: Alive, and feeling better.

Diction, sound, and words compose my way.
Without, the house would be in disarray.
Today I moved your journals to the hall,
Last night I collaged our bedroom wall.

Abe, remember our gazebo in the yard?
I painted it with pictures of the bard.
Come to me, listen, Sweet, to the bird's song.
Just a minute, sit with me, not for long.

We'll read *Shalom Aleichem* in the shade,
snuggle like we used to. Then go, my Abe.

November 3, 2011

No other subject is as compelling

When I was caring for Abe, writing was the one activity that helped me identify caregiving problems. Writing helped me express feelings about our changed relationship and about my changing relationships with family members and friends. Writing also helped me understand what was going on with my own health issues.

I'm still writing about him. I can't seem to break away. No other subject is as compelling. The Alzheimer's years hold me. Will I ever get back to my real work? Or is this it?

November 4, 2011

He was the family photographer

I might as well be on an archeological dig the way I'm scrambling through the house looking for photos of him. The photo hunt is a major component of my healing process. Problem is, Abe was the family photographer, so I have more photos with him behind the camera than in front of it. I've dug up some treasures, though and am scanning them into the computer. Maybe I'll want to put them in a book someday.

November 19, 2011

Missing

It's seventeen months
since you've been gone
and I still miss your skin.
I search for you
as if you were
a phantom,
a doppelgänger
or a lost limb.
It's seventeen months
since you've been gone
and I still miss your skin.
I search for you
as if you were
a phantom,
a doppelgänger
or a lost limb.
How many times can I say it—
I miss your skin.

November 24, 2011

As a doctor he examined the body.
As a pathologist,
he examined the body even more closely
than other doctors.
He knew the parts of the body
as well as he knew the names of fruits and vegetables.
Often I asked him questions of science
and he answered kindly,
without reservation or academic elitism.
He was a real teacher, a mensch.
One time before we knew he was sick
I asked him the name of a bone in the body.
(I've forgotten which one)
and he stared at me, with a gape almost,
as if I were asking him a question
from a foreign universe.
Every muscle in his body
relaxed, his mind wandering
into not knowing what he always knew.
He worked on every bone,
damn it. I know it's Thanksgiving,
and I should feel grateful
but I don't, at least not
for Alzheimer's.

December 27, 2011

Let There Be Light & A Little Less Confusion Here

I don't come from a religious family. My parents were Leftists, and as conflicted as that segment of the Jewish population is, they sent me and my sister to an Orthodox Sunday school—Shaarei Zion, in Lower Park Heights, Baltimore. My brother fared less well (or better); he had to go kicking and screaming to a real Hebrew School—Isaac Davidson— three times a week.

When my teachers, Rabbi Tabak's daughters, asked me why my parents didn't keep kosher, I was embarrassed but didn't answer. I knew the reason had something to do with the secrets some families kept during the McCarthy era.

Mother gave in to Chanukah lighting candles. She bought a box from Press's kosher grocery store —we lived upstairs—and took out a tin cake pan. We lit the bottom of the candles so they'd stick to the pan, and every night (or maybe it was most every night) my sister and I lit candles with Mother standing over us, always a confused look on her face. I don't remember my brother and father being present at this lighting ceremony. Only the women folk. When my Aunt Fanny was there, she gave us each a quarter for Chanukah *gelt*.

By the time my classmates started preparing for Bat Mitvah lessons, which in the Orthodox tradition took place at age twelve, I rebelled. By that time I was confused enough to know that something wasn't just right with this faith vs. politics thing. Both my sister and I said we didn't want to go to Sunday school any more.

2012

January 2, 2012

Aging in the digital age

When Abe retired in 1996, he spoke about getting a Macintosh. That's what we called Macs in the old days. I reverted to the original term recently when I bought myself a 13" MacBook Air. My daughter laughed: "I haven't heard Macs called that in a long time," she said. Probably not since 1997 when Steve Jobs developed the Mac OS 8 and certainly not since 1998 when the iMac came on the market. Nonetheless, I reverted to *Macintosh* and recalled the day when Abe and I went into the Apple store to begin his search for the just-right-computer. I had been using a PC since 1985 and wasn't interested in going over to Apple, which didn't happen until last month, but I was anxious, at the time, to see Abe put one into action.

Before his retirement in 1996, Abe didn't want to go near a computer. He had watched me at my PC for over ten years yet didn't try a hand at it himself. This was around the time when Group Health, where Abe worked, was computerizing files, and staff would soon be learning to use the new digital system. Abe was an old-fashioned doc. He read medical journals, researched his cases in the library, sat at his microscope and recorded his findings. Once Group Health went digital, he said, *Ok, it's time,* and he closed up shop. So when he said: *I think I'll buy myself a Macintosh,* I couldn't have been more pleased.

We spent about an hour in the Apple store having fun fiddling with the computers. "So which one are we getting?" I ask him. He shrugs his shoulders: *I'll think about it for a while.* "Hmmm," I say to myself. When we get home, he picks up the newspaper. A few days later

I get him to go to the Apple store again. We fiddle with the computers. "So which one do you like?" I ask. *I'll sit on the idea for a while,* he says

The following week, we make another trip to the Apple store. Same thing. He might as well have been researching one of his cases. We go home, and he picks up his newspaper. Ok, so I'm getting the picture. This is not going to happen—not now, not ever. No more than my dream to go to the moon is going to happen.

Abe never got a Macintosh or any other kind of computer. He never sat at one, except when on those "shopping sprees." He didn't really want a computer, though he did like the idea of knowing how to use one—had he been another person. Computers turn us into different people. They turn us into who we are not and maybe who we weren't born to be. Abe wasn't born to use a computer and deep down he knew it. He couldn't be other than who he always was, and I'm glad—and not glad. Had his brain allowed him to move beyond his old self maybe he would have stayed healthier longer. Maybe he might have even lived longer had he learned to use a computer.

I'm learning how to use my new MacBook Air. It's often frustrating and I can see why some of my generation, who weren't raised with computers, push the whole thing away. I'm also learning to use iWork Pages, for me a new word processing program. It's not easy, but I refuse to give up—at least at this point. Not that Abe gave up on computers; they just weren't his style. As for me, I seem to have become immersed enough in the digital age so that yesterday when my niece asked me to send her my address, I sent her my url. It took me another email to realize she wanted my "land" address.

March 7, 2012

It doesn't matter if they know you, visit

This morning I went to an Alzheimer's Association fundraiser at the downtown Hyatt Hotel. I rarely go to such events, but a board member invited me to sit at his table, and it's such a trustworthy organization, I went. This was a big deal for me because at 7:30 a.m. I do absolutely nothing outside my house except take care of Emma. If I'm still inside at that time, I'm reading or writing or trying to guess two or three words of a crossword puzzle.

I'm glad I went. It was good to hear people speaking publicly about Alzheimer's and to be in a room with over 400 people giving their time, energy and money to research a disease that, in my daughter's words, kicks people in the knees and doesn't let them up.

The wonderful Connie Thompson of KOMO 4 News spoke about caring for her mom. The artist, Kevan Atteberry, talked about caring for his wife, Teri, who has early-onset Alzheimer's. These two described what I know too well—life in extremity, where no matter what one does, the loved one will not get better.

When I came home, I talked on the phone to my daughter and, then, I walked Emma. A few blocks into our walk, I ran into an acquaintance. We got to talking about Alzheimer's. (It's been a year and nine months and I still don't know what else to talk about). She asked me: "Did he know you?" I told her what I tell everyone who asks me that question: "It didn't matter if he knew me. He smiled when I came in. I made him happy."

People with Alzheimer's may not remember who you are, but they feel your presence. They know you're there. Sit with them. Hold her hand. Scratch his back. Visit. They need you.

March 9, 2012

He was never a shadow to me

I normally don't use the word "soul," but I will today because I'm trying to understand why people use the word "shadow" to describe what happens to the Alzheimer's patient as he or she begins losing memory and functionality.

Let's say there is such a thing as a soul, a fundamental essence, some-thing that's always within a person, regardless of what happens to him or to her on the outside—in terms of looks, behavior, or circumstance.

Let's say we meet someone in life whose soul touches ours so deeply that even if the two don't always understand each other on a day-to-day basis or get along with one another all the time, something inside of each stays connected with the other.

Let's say one of these people gets sick in such a way that most people don't understand him anymore. Little by little this sick person loses his knowledge about the past, about who people are, what his relationship was with them, even with his wife and children.

Let's say he's even forgotten what position he held in the world. In fact, one day he asks his wife: *What kind of business was I in?* His wife says: "You were a doctor." *A doctor?* he asks in surprise. "Yes, you were a doctor." *That's nice*, he says, and goes back to looking at a pic-ture book.

Would you say that this man is a shadow of his former self? I wouldn't. I'd say he was stricken with a disease that erased his memory and that this erasure stripped him of the capacity to live life the way he used to. He is not a shadow. He is who he always was; he's just living differently now. His outside self, the one the world sees, has changed, but the inner self, call it a soul, is there. Take time to look. If you choose not to, or if you can't, that doesn't mean you're looking at a shadow.

I never saw Abe as a shadow of a former self. To me, he was Abe until the moment he died. He might have lost his memory, his executive skills, body movements and a host of other things, but if there is such a thing as a soul, Abe's was intact.

We're all looking for the "right" way to be around Alzheimer's. We're searching for appropriate words to use, but language is difficult. We need to choose words that don't diminish a person's essence, that don't make him or her less on the inside than he or she still is. This morning's *New York Times* included an article about the writer Jeanette Winterspoon. She writes: "Whatever is on the outside can be taken away at any time. Only what is inside you is safe." We need to keep people diagnosed with Alzheimer's safe, especially from humiliation. People living with Alzheimer's are not shadows. Let's not make them so.

March 10, 2012

A Bronx High School of Science classmate writes to me

"In addition to his superior intellect Abe Schweid was a kind and thoughtful man. I wish there were multiple clones of him in his prime. I once encountered Abe several years after we graduated and I still remember how he took the time to inquire how my life was going. It was not going well at the time but his words of encouragement cheered me up." RE

June 15, 2012

Second year

This second year after Abe's death
my body hurts all the time.
Feet talk back to me
I can hardly get a word in.

Knees are rocks
that weigh me to my chair.
Elbows yell for Ibuprofen.
Lower back wants some too.

My body hurts all the time
I can hardly get a word in.

Exercise taunts me
to take advantage of possibilities
at the YWCA, Curves, Seattle Health Club,
Meadowbrook swimming pool.

But I look Exercise in the eye,
say, I'm doing just fine
and though I think about it sometimes
mostly I just go back to sleep.

September 18, 2012

I need to let Abe rest in peace

After three years, I've put the blog to rest. I hope it helped others as much as it did me. But it's time for me to stop writing about Alzheimer's. I need to let Abe rest in peace, and I have to let "us" be all of who we were together—and nothing more.

Writing has been my vehicle for documenting my journey with Abe through Alzheimer's Disease. It has also been a place for me to contain my grief; it still is. Certainly the events of the days described here would not have remained present to me had I not jotted down these entries. Words on the page (or the screen) are the only way I know how to keep "us" with me, even if "us" is merely a representation of "us."

I say "representation" because no matter how close we think we have gotten to the truth, the page (or the screen) is never the real thing. In that sense, all writing is a lie. Memory and truth change when removed from the geographic and temporal proximity of the event. When I reread these poems and diary entries I know I was honest in the moment of writing; and all that I have included holds true for me in this moment. This will change over time, certainly.

Epilogue

Recently, I was asked how my life has changed since Abe died. My first response was that it hasn't changed and yet I know that can't be. Initially, I thought I would continue visiting the nursing home, to see the patients and staff I had "grown up with," as some do after their loved ones die. I did go twice but became too sad and didn't go back anymore. I admire the widows and widowers who do return, even signing up to volunteer, but, after Abe's stint and my mother's before him, I need a rest. I've joined an organization concerned with compassionate dying, and I hope I have the wherewithal to end my life on my own terms when it's time. I have a feeling though that, like most people, I won't have a choice. And if I don't have that choice and have to go to a nursing home, I hope that the people who are assigned to care for me are as filled with as much compassion as those who cared for Abe. My diary reminds me that I have been worried about this for some time. In 2010, I wrote the poem:

Who will care for me?

If I end up dying
the way he did
who will care for me
but nursing home attendants
from Somalia,
Ethiopia
and Eritrea,
countries I've
only read about
until now

their people
handling my husband,
as if to anoint him.
"My family is in Eritrea,"
she says
while adjusting the pillow
behind Abe's head.
She comes to him in prayer,
I think, as if he were an altar
a place of worship.
She seems to bless him
as if he were her Grandpa.
"He is my family now,"
she says,
and I believe her.

I thought that after Abe died I might move to Israel where my child-hood family lives, but the United States is my homeland, not *eretz yisrael*. I might have become more active in the synagogue where Abe and I met in 1981; but I cried when I went in. Eventually I resigned. Synagogue life wasn't something I grew up with. I went there to hear Abe's voice and my grandfather's and to live inside my old neighbor-hood, the *shtetl* in Baltimore where I grew up. That neighborhood no longer exists though, and I no longer want to use a *shul* to remember. My remembering takes place on the page, which is where I am most days and nights. Now I have as much time as I want to sit at the computer and write and enough time to read the way I like. In December I read thirty-one books of poetry, one for each day of my birthday month. That was my present to myself. All the while, Abe sat with me. The 2010 diary reminds me:

He's on my shoulder

Sometimes I find him sitting on my right shoulder.
It's soothing to have him there.
He doesn't say anything, and I don't say anything.
He just sits with me. It's kind of fun, really.
I mentioned that I was having a hard time getting his gravestone up.
I think I've figured out why.
I thought that once the gravestone was up,
I'd have to remove him from my shoulder
but maybe I don't.
He can sit there as long as he wants,
after all. Aren't I in charge of this narrative?

Time for change hasn't come for me yet, no matter how others may want to rush me. I need to recollect myself in today's world and figure out where I want to step next. In the meantime, as I meet new people, I look back on the years Abe and I spent together, and I'm grateful for all of them. A final note: I asked one of Abe's doctor friends, Rick Rapport, if he thought I was betraying Abe in writing this story. He said: "Of course not! People die in two ways. The first they stop breathing. The second is when the last person speaks his name." I hope many people speak the name "Abe Schweid" and keep it alive for a very long time. He was valiant.

Esther Altshul Helfgott
Seattle
February, 2013

About the Author

Esther Altshul Helfgott is a nonfiction writer and poet with a Ph.D. in history from the University of Washington. Her work appears in the *Journal of Poetry Therapy, Maggid: A Journal of Jewish Literature, Drash: Northwest Mosaic, American Imago: Psychoanalysis and the Human Sciences, Raven Chronicles, Floating Bridge Review. Beyond Forgetting: Poetry and Prose about Alzheimer's Disease, Jack Straw Anthology, Blue Lyra Revie, HistoryLink*, and elsewhere. She is a longtime literary activist, a 2010 Jack Straw poet, and the founder of Seattle's "It's About Time Writer's Reading Series," now in its 23nd year. She is the author of the *The Homeless One: A Poem in Many Voices* (Kota, 2000), a poetic docu-drama about schizophrenia and homelessness, which has been performed as a play. For three years, Esther wrote the blog "Witnessing Alzheimer's: A Caregiver's View," for the Seattle Post-Intelligencer online. Her wish is that young people get to know their grandparents, and hold their hands. www.estherhelfgott.com

About Penny Harvest

The Common Cents Penny Harvest grew from one child's desire to feed the homeless, and since 1991, children between the ages of four and 14 have been converting their natural compassion for others into action by collecting pennies and turning those pennies into grants for community organizations—$8.1 million in grants donated by children since 1991! The Penny Harvest shows young people they have the ability to make the world a better place by introducing them to the power of philanthropy and service during their formative years. As children help others, they develop their generosity and moral character, and they learn through practice the skills and responsibilities of democratic participation. Principals and parents find that the Penny Harvest encourages a caring culture and sense of belonging; teachers see it as an an opportunity to enhance curriculum through a blend of service-learning, character education, and child philanthropy; community leaders value the millions of dollars and hours that children donate back to better our communities; and kids like the program because it's fun! http://www.commoncents.org/ go/penny-harvest/ about-the-penny-harvest

Acknowledgments

Our Children
The Schweids - Sabrina,Wynne, Lisa, Erich
The Helfgotts – Jackie, Ian, Scott, Bernard, Zach, Sue

Our Grandchildren
Zach, Hunter, Zalia, Aaron, Ray

Alzheimer's Association
Congregation Beth Shalom
Foss Nursing Home
Group Health Hospital
Jack Straw Productions

Poeming the Silence Writing Class
Mildred Andrews, Karen Baker, Carolyn Cox, Rebecca Crichton,
Pat Gunn, Nikki Norstrom, Micky Yeary

Women's Writing Group
Katy Ellis, Ann B. Hursey, Ruby Murray, Denise Calvetti Michaels,
Ann Teplick

It's About Time Writers' Reading Series
Peggy Sturdivant, Katie Tynan

Jeannine Hall Gailey, Judy Neuman, Hillel Kieval, Rabbi Billy Altshul,
Moshe Schorr

Kelli Russell Agodon

Tanya Johnson and Douglas P. Johnson, Publisher
Cave Moon Press

Publications

"Alzheimer Couple"—*Northwest Prime Time,* Alzheimer's issue, Nov. 2006

"An Alzheimer Marriage"—*Northwest Prime Time,* Alzheimer's issue, Nov 2007

"No Pits"—*Centrifugal Eye,* Summer 2006

"Suzzallo"—*Seattle Writergrrls Uncapped,* Spring 2006

"Living with Alzheimer's - The Almost Widow"—*Northwest Prime Time,* Nov. 2006

"Writing and the Alzheimer's Caregiver"—*Centrifugal Eye,* Summer 2006

"The Old Pathologist"—*Chrysanthemum,* 2006

"Laboratory Visit"—*Chrysanthemum,* 2006

"There's Tenderness in Bananas: Reflections on A New Year" —*JT News,* September 30, 2005

"Mary Oliver's Bone"—*The Museletter: News and Resources from the National Association of Poetry Therapy,* July 2006, p. 36

"Caregiver's Village Not Big Enough"—*Seattle P.I.,* August 13, 2007

Spouse as Home, Beyond Forgetting: Poetry and Prose about Alzheimer's Disease. Holly Hughes, ed. (Kent State University Press) 2009

"Witnessing Alzheimer's through Diary and Poem - Dear Alzheimer's: Why Did You Pick Our Sheltered Lives to Visit?" *The Journal of Poetry Therapy*, Winter 2009

"Diary of My Husband's Illness: After His Death - Still Witnessing Alzheimer's," *The Journal of Poetry Therapy*, Fall 2011

"Blog - Witnessing Alzheimer's: A Caregiver's View," *Seattle Post-Intelligencer*, Nov. 28, 2008 – 2012

"You Can Improve the Quality of Life for Alzheimer's Patients" —*Seattle P.I.*, June 13, 2007

"Fragments from an Alzheimer's Journey"—*FragLit Journal*, Fall 2009 Reprinted in Jack Straw Anthology, 2010; Floating Bridge *Review* 4, Summer 2011